The New Women of Color Daily Devotional · *Winter Edition*

The articles and prayers are taken from the *Women of Color Devotional Bible* © World Bible / Nia Publishing Co.

© Urban Spirit! Publishing and Media Company is an African American owned company based in Atlanta, GA. You can find more information at http://www.urbanspirit.biz/

The New Women of Color Daily Devotional · Winter Edition © Urban Spirit! Publishing and Media Company

Produced with the assistance of Cheryl Wilson, i4Details and Larry Taylor, LTD2

All Scripture quotes, unless otherwise indicated, are from the Authorized King James Version of the Bible.

Scripture quotes marked Amplified are from the Amplified Bible, © Copyright 1954, 1958, 1962, 1964, 1965, 1987 by The Lockman Foundation.

Scripture quotes marked NASB are taken from the New American Standard Bible® Copyright © 1960, 1962, 1963, 1968, 1971, 1972, 1973, 1975, 1977, 1995 by The Lockman Foundation.

Scripture quotes marked NIV are taken from the HOLY BIBLE, NEW INTERNATIONAL VERSION®. Copyright© 1973, 1978, 1984 by the International Bible Society.

Scripture quotes marked NLT are taken from the Holy Bible, New Living Translation, copyright © 1996. Used by permission of Tyndale House Publishers, Inc, Wheaton, Illinois 60189. All rights reserved.

Manufactured in the United States of America

WOMEN COLOR
DAILY DEVOTIONAL

DECEMBER - JANUARY - FEBRUARY

TABLE OF
CONTENTS

Dear Sister,

Harvest time is a wonderful season for you to plant seeds of faith by strengthening your Christian walk. Winter is also the impeccable time not only to cozy up to a fire, but also to warm your heart and soul with the love of Jesus. Twenty-six fabulous women from all over the country have written devotionals (devos) that address significant themes for these seasons.

The aim of this book is for you to dig daily into the devos and allow them to be the spark to help you grow even nearer to our Lord. Each devo has a title, a thought-provoking question, a scripture, a short story, an application, and a closing prayer. When positioned together into a daily devotional, the mixture is a tool to help you prod deeper into the Word.

It is our desire that the words on each page speak to your spirit. May your journey during the months of September through February bring you peace, hope, faith, and the understanding that the Lord is with you, no matter the month or season.

God bless,

Stephanie Perry Moore
General Editor

DECEMBER
WEEK 1

DAY 1
OPEN EARS

Did you listen to the Holy Spirit?

"Better it is to be of an humble spirit with the lowly, listen to the spirit than to divide the spoil with the proud."
(PROVERBS 16:19)

STORY

On a cool spring day in March, Carrie and Eula arrived early for their annual conference in Sacramento, California. The women checked into their hotel, went to their room, dropped their bags, and then headed to the mall located next to the hotel. Carrie headed to the bookstore because she loved to read. Eula went with her. Carrie quickly spotted two books that she wanted to purchase and read. Eula said she would just read one of Carrie's books. The women returned to their hotel room and put away their clothing so that they could prepare to read.

Carrie permitted Eula to read the book of her choice. Eula chose the book titled, *In Ten Days Your Life Will Change*. That book sparked her interest. All she could think about was her expectation that in the next ten days, she would surely get a large sum of money. The book stated that if you read the 23rd Psalm five times a day—upon waking up, breakfast, lunch, dinner, and bedtime—after ten days your life will change. Eula was excited and religiously read the scripture passage daily as she could hardly wait for the tenth day to come and go.

APPLICATION

The Holy Spirit is the third person of the trinity: God the Father, Jesus the Son, and the Holy Spirit. The Spirit is there for you to seek guidance, but you must trust the Spirit to direct you properly. Whenever you are about to take on any task, you should first ask God to order your steps. When God orders your steps, you are able to set aside personal pride and listen to His directions so that you can hear what He is saying to you. It is always necessary to be still for a moment. You will need to exercise humility and faith to know that God is directing you, not your own thoughts. You cannot be full of self-pride, which will prevent the Spirit from taking over.

Please remember that only the Holy Spirit can guide you to open your ears to hear God. Sometimes, you attribute worldly thoughts and actions as those that the Spirit has instilled or directed. God wants you to know that He directs the Spirit to lead you to your thought and actions. Never be too quick to jump and do things that you think are right rather than listen to Him, so that you will know that there is a message in all that the Spirit directs you to do.

P R A Y E R

Heavenly Father, I come to thank You first for allowing me to be your child, for giving me the mind to seek You for directions and for sending the Spirit to humble me to be still and open my ears to hear what You are saying to me. Dear God, I know that only You can hold my hands and lead me through the thickness of whatever I may face, not allowing me to stumble and fall. Dear God, please let Your voice be so distinct that I may not mistake any other voice for Yours. Father, I beg you to allow your Spirit to dwell upon me so that my path will be clear, and Your Word will abide in me today and always. Amen.

KNOW IT

Do you recognize the touch?

*"But God who is rich in mercy,
for his great love wherewith he loved us."*
(EPHESIAN 2:4)

STORY

Eula excitedly faced the eleventh day. She realized that the day did not end until 11:59 p.m. that night. Eula thought to herself that nothing had changed. On day twelve, Eula followed the same routine as day eleven. On day thirteen, Eula faced the day with the attitude that what she read had no truth to it. The mother of an adult son who had moved to Houston and a

teenage daughter still at home, little did Eula know that a change had already occurred in her life.

Eula felt a bit tired, so she did not go to Bible study with her husband; instead, she picked up her daughter from tutoring so that she could go to bed early. At 9 p.m., the phone rang, and Eula answered in a voice that implied, "I don't want to talk." Yet, the person on the other end continued to speak. Eula tearfully searched for a pen and wrote down the information that the person gave her. She was in disbelief that her son Lee had been killed. She frantically called out for her daughter to come quickly. Her frightened daughter heard her mother scream, "Lord have mercy on me!"

APPLICATION

Many times, the Lord has touched you and covered you with mercy, yet you do not know it. Mercy is God's undeserving gift to you and His forgiveness for your wrong doings. God's mercy brings us to a life-changing understanding that His love will carry us through all adversities.

When God's children call out to Him, He is there waiting to provide their needs. God is there when you feel numb to His touch and when you cannot speak the words to call on Him. God can and will extend His mercy to you just as He did to Joseph's brothers who threw him in a hole. We can see that God's mercy is endless. His unmerited favor is available to all who believe in Him.

There comes a time when all you can do is accept the fact that God's mercy is great, and as a result, you should be ready to forgive and extend mercy to others as God has done for you. He is faithful and keeps his promises from generation to generation to his children who keep His commandments. One might ask the question, "How can a God who says He is a jealous God continue to extend His mercy over and over again?" He will do this because of His unceasing love and promise never to forsake us.

PRAYER

Dear God, thank You for Your many blessings. Thank You for the undeserving acts of love and mercy. God, there are times when I am so burdened down that the words won't come, and all I can do is call out, "Lord have mercy on me." Father God, You know and see what Your children need. Please manifest Yourself today and show Your mercy toward your children. Lord, I recognize that Your mercy is a free will gift and many times, it may appear as if it is unappreciated, but please overlook my shortcomings as You demonstrate Your mercy towards me. Father God, I know that a plea for Your mercy is sometimes asking You to forgive my sins and grant Your love that I do not deserve. In the name of Your son Jesus, I pray, Amen.

DAY 3
IT HURTS

Where are you?

*"Let us therefore come boldly unto the throne of grace,
that we may obtain mercy,
and find grace to help in time of need."*

(HEBREWS 4:16)

STORY

With eyes full of tears, Eula instructed her frightened daughter to make a call to her aunt in Houston to tell her that her favorite nephew Lee had been killed. Eula did not call to inform her husband since it was almost time for him to arrive home. Eula got enough strength to call Carrie. Carrie said they would be right there in spite of Eula saying, "That's okay." In her spirit, she was hoping Carrie was already there. The next call was to her preacher friend and her son's godmother. In between consoling her daughter and making phone calls, by the time her husband arrived at home, the house was filled with family and friends. The house remained that way throughout the following week.

The coroner told Eula the family could not view her son's body for identification and that dental records would be the determining source. This sent Eula into a tailspin. Her husband flew to Houston, hoping to view the body but to no avail. He arranged for the body to fly home to Los Angeles. In the meantime, Eula's pastor and Lee's godmother went with her to the mortuary to make funeral arrangements.

APPLICATION

Grace is God's unmerited favor, which we all need. Grace is also God's gift that He gives to His children. It is an expression of God's love for you. It is extended to the just and unjust. Grace will carry you through all situations. You can say, "Lord have mercy," and He will exercise His grace. In times when you do not know which way to turn, He is there to cover you with His grace. God will allow his grace to prevail when you do not seem to know what to say or how to say what you need. God is always there to cover you in his grace.

It is the grace of God that gives you the simple things in life that you may think are automatic. They are not. They are the result of the grace of God. God already knows that you cannot do it on your own no matter how minimal you may think the task is. Little do you know that God is there waiting on you to call on Him, and He will be there. He knows that you cannot do anything on your own. God's grace will catch your tears, calm your shaking hands, strengthen your weak legs, put running in your feet and love in your heart. His grace will provide all your essential needs, even when you fail to ask or acknowledge Him.

PRAYER

Oh, Lamb of God, my rock in a weary land, my comforter in a time of storms, and my Savior, please let Your grace fall down on me and cover me with a blanket of Your love. Father, I am like a child in a maze, every direction that I turn I cannot seem to find my way. Oh, God, please shower me with Your mercy and grace. I am in pain; I am badly hurt. A part of me is gone, and I feel as though I cannot go any further. Heavenly Father, cover me with Your love as I surrender all to You. Lord, I know that You are there, so please answer me. I need You to continue to cover me with Your love and grace. Lord, I will continue to praise Your holy name, Amen.

DAY 4
CAN'T STAND

Where is the prop?

*"And he said unto her, Daughter, be of good comfort:
thy faith hath made thee whole; go in peace."*
(LUKE 8:48)

STORY

Eula was terrified of going to the mortuary, as
this was the first time that she had to handle
such a task. After arriving there, she began to
get weak and tearful. Her pastor told her to go
downstairs, and he would negotiate the cost.
When her pastor finished the business part, he
called for Eula to come and choose a casket. She
was shaking and saying, "God you promised never
to leave me, and I need you." In her spirit, she
could hear, "Oh, you of little faith." Eula dried her

eyes and told the counselor she was ready to finalize her son's funeral.

After arriving back home, Eula began searching for pictures and met with Mrs. Yolanda, who was writing the obituary and preparing the funeral program. By night, the house was full again with people bringing all sorts of food, but Eula did not eat and had not eaten since the night before. Somehow, she managed to get through the evening, hoping that her husband would soon get home. The next day was Good Friday, but she failed to find anything good in the fact that her son's body was arriving in Los Angeles for funeral preparation.

APPLICATION

Many times, we are overcome by fatigue or some sort of pain in the body that brings on weakness. However, when we suffer emotional weakness brought on by the death of a loved one, it is an unfamiliar kind of weakness. At this crisis in life, it is a time to exercise faith in God that will see you through this traumatic experience. It is important not to think of what little faith that you may have but rather to believe that you have a leaning post that will never let you fall. This post will not even tilt but stand strong and support you before you fall. It will hold you up. For this to happen, you must have faith that can be as small as a mustard seed.

God reminds you that you must walk by faith and not by sight when you are trusting in Him to be right there. Evidence of having faith is facing devastating issues and challenges while maintaining sufficient strength to bring whatever you are facing to a conclusion. Putting it simply, faith is believing God will supply whatever you need, when you need it. People put their money in the bank for safekeeping. When they go back to the bank to get some of their money, they expect the bank to have their money available because they have faith in that bank.

PRAYER

Gracious and everlasting Father, please allow Your spirit to abide in me so that I may be able to stand. I am weak, Lord, and I do not seem to know what to say, do or how to handle this devastating crisis in my life. I do not want to fall, Lord, because so many are depending on me, but I am trembling, weak and scared. I need your help. Father, Peter's faith allowed him to walk on water until he started to doubt; God, I am so afraid that I cannot even take the first step. God, help me to stand on my belief that my faith in You is the reality of things not seen. Lord, this blessing I ask in Your precious son Jesus' name, Amen.

DAY 5
HANDS UP

Can you Smile?

*"I will praise thee, O Lord, with my whole heart;
I will shew forth all thy marvellous works."*
(PSALM 9:1)

STORY

Eula made it through the funeral, but she was exhausted. In a few days, all of the family was gone, and her husband was on a trip to Spain, so she was alone. Carrie checked on her daily, and her friend Rose spent the night with her. Eula dreaded going back to work. As she feared, on her first day back to work, she fell apart. Her supervisor told her not to worry and to go home for the day.

Flowers came for weeks but seeing them was bittersweet. Eula had accepted that she would walk around forever with a hole in her stomach from the loss of her son.

One morning, at the request of a sorority sister, she went to the mirror and looked at herself. Her sorority sister asked if she liked what she saw. Eula said, "No." Her sorority sister told her to point at the mirror and say, as if she really meant it, "Satan you are a liar. You will not take my joy away. The Lord gives and He takes away. Lee was mine for a season."

Once Eula began to believe these words, she was able to move forward in her life. Now, she spends lots of time sharing with other mothers on how to get through losing a child.

APPLICATION

Praise is what you should do. You should lift your eyes to the hills from where your help comes. Indeed, it comes from the Lord. You may think that it is other people, but it was God who used those people to be there for you. When God heals your body or provides your needs through whatever vehicle that He chooses to use, you are to give Him all the praise and honor.

Praise is lifting up the name of God for who He is and what He has done. An expression of your gratefulness is telling others that your God had mercy upon you, pulled you out of a pit, and gave you a message to tell others. He has given you a voice to tell of His goodness, His mercy, and His grace to all those who put their trust in His son Jesus Christ. Praising God in sincerity shows gratitude for what He has done for you. Praise him through songs, in your prayers, and in your fellowship with believers.

Remember, God will never send you out empty handed; He will always equip you with what to say and to whom. Sometimes, God will allow a crisis in your life and then see you through it so that you might lift up His name in praise for what He has done. Hallelujah is the highest praise we can give God. This praise should always be on our lips.

PRAYER

My heavenly Father, I come to You with praise on my lips and thanksgiving in my heart, asking You for Your grace and mercy to cover me day in and day out. Lord, I will be so careful to give You all the praise and honor. I thank You, God, for another day's journey. I thank You for so many examples of Your love for me. Lord, I praise You for the air that I breathe, the sun that shines, the water that comes down from the skies, the moon and stars, as well as the cattle on a thousand hills. Father God, I thank You for the believers that You placed in my path as well as those lives that You prepared me to touch through ministry. Oh Lord, I thank You for preparing my heart for me to be able to give You an abundance of praise. Amen.

DECEMBER
WEEK 2

DAY 1
MERCY AND NO FAITH

Are you ready to go where God leads you?

*"And the Lord shall guide thee continually,
and satisfy thy soul in drought, and make fat thy bones:
and thou shalt be like a watered garden,
and like a spring of water, whose waters fail not."*
(ISAIAH 58:11)

STORY

On a glooming Sunday morning, with a midst of soft rain beginning to sprinkle, Tammy and her husband, Sam, loaded the last of their possessions into the moving van. The time had come for them to step out in faith as her husband had accepted a new job. The job was taking them

twenty-five hundred miles away from the closet family member.

After one year of marriage and work in lower paying jobs, they received an awesome opportunity. Sam accepted a position to coach at a big Division I school, and she did not have to work outside of home. Though this was great, they still had reservations as to why God was sending them so far away from home. They cried as they backed out of our driveway, knowing that they were about to journey into unknown territory. Tammy knew this job was the answer to her prayer for them to have more benefits and more income. She and Sam knew having additional money could help them start a family.

Though Tammy was not specific in her request, God granted the wish. It was up to her to decide how to embrace it. They traveled for two days before they reached their assigned destination. They sat in the hotel parking lot and prayed, thanking God for giving them traveling grace and for keeping them out of harm's way. Before she got out of the van, she looked at Sam and said, "What are we doing?" Sam smiled and replied, "We have faith in God." She knew they were out of their comfort zone, but they were ready to take on the task.

APPLICATION

Sometimes, you might question God when you find yourself in an uncertain place. Nevertheless, when you look at tough situations as your assignment from God and know that His mercy will not give you more than you can bear, you are better able to tackle the tough spots of life. God loves you and when you feel put to the test, realize that His grace covers you. If you are being pushed, it is to move you to greatness. If you are going through the fire, it is to come out as pure gold. If you feel pressed down, it is to get you ready to soar.

Being a child of the most high God, understand that you have grit and grind to make it through the journey. Continue to pray and ask God to lead and guide you. Stand on faith, and trust that He is with you as you walk in His will.

Leave all your fears behind. Be grateful for the opportunity God gives. Make the best of every situation. Remain thankful and stay focused on Him. Always allow God to lead and guide you.

PRAYER

Father, I thank You for all the blessings You have stored before me, those seen and unseen. I know there is no me or we if there is no You. I thank You. I pray You will always allow me to know and see that I am where You want me to be. It is by Your grace and mercy that I have been given all opportunities in this life. Lord, help me to be content with the things that I have and to be satisfied with the blessings You have given me. For it is in Jesus' name, I pray, Amen.

DAY 2
MERCY AND NO OBEDIENCE

Are you able to focus on the task?

*"And the world passeth away, and the lust thereof:
but he that doeth the will of God abideth for ever."*
(I JOHN 2:17)

STORY

Tammy and Sam were in a new town. Sam's job was going well so far. They adjusted to their new environment, hoping to get to know their neighbors. Tammy noticed that though the people were friendly, they seemed to stare as if she and Sam were out of place and did not belong. This made Tammy feel somewhat uncomfortable.

As time went by, a neighbor finally mustered up the nerve to ask her what brought them to Utah. Tammy shared that her husband was a position coach for the university. The neighbor was very excited and thrilled to have a coach in the neighborhood. The city was small, and football was all there was for weekend entertainment.

Days passed and Tammy began to get invites to the different social gatherings the women were having. Being the only minority there, she felt a tad out of place, and she was not sure if they liked her for her. Tammy was torn about whether to let her guard down. However, she felt her spirit say, "Relax and enjoy." She just did not know if she could obey.

APPLICATION

You must always keep doubt as far away as possible and never let it from creep in your mind. Remember that the devil is busy, but know that the assignment was a blessing from God. When you feel unsettled and doubtful, it is time for you to find a prayer closet to cast all your concerns and fears before Him.

You must know it is okay to feel lonely and down, but just remember that He is who He says He is. There is no circumstance, problem, or situation that God cannot handle. Just allow Him to use you.

PRAYER

Father, I thank You for never leaving me nor forsaking me during my lowest and weakest time. I realize You are in control and You never put more on me than I can bear. I pray that You will always allow me to believe and know that You are in control of every challenge and situation that comes my way. Thank You for allowing me to trust and believe and to remain obedient always. In Jesus' name, Amen.

DAY 3
MERCY AND NO GRACE

Are you able to accept God's grace?

"And he said unto me, My grace is sufficient for thee: for my strength is made perfect in weakness. Most gladly therefore will I rather glory in my infirmities, that the power of Christ may rest upon me."

(II CORINTHIANS 12:9)

STORY

Tammy found out she was pregnant. Though overjoyed, she was worried because she did not have her mother close. She then realized that her new friends were there to help and be like her family. This was an extra blessing because her husband worked long hours. Tammy was so

thankful she had obeyed God and gotten to know other believers in her area.

The closer the due date came, the more Tammy became frazzled. She began bugging her husband about him being away. While he could not help that he had to work, they argued more.

The due date had passed, and Tammy was beginning to experience some complications. Her doctor stated that if the baby did not come in a few days, he would have to induce. The next day her water broke, and she found herself in the emergency room about to bring another life into the world. She was in labor for twelve hours before having to have a C-section due to complications. It was then that she repented for being so angry and asked for grace. She also asked for Sam's forgiveness. He kissed her and granted it. She only prayed that the Lord would too.

APPLICATION

People are not perfect. We do not deserve God's many blessings. However, you can look deep into your heart and ask God to give you a right spirit. Seek His grace so you can be right with those you have hurt.

Trials and tribulations can weigh us down and cause us to stumble. However, God's grace and mercy can bring you through it all. Focus on Him in times of trouble and know that He will get you to a better place.

PRAYER

Father, I know it was You and only You who allowed things to happen in the order they took place. I thank You for removing me out of my own way so that I could allow You to do Your work in me. Father, I pray that You will continue to guide me through whatever lies ahead. I know that only your grace will carry me through this life. In Jesus' name, Amen.

DAY 4
MERCY AND NO CHARITY

Are you being a blessing to someone else?

*"And above all these things put on charity,
which the bond of perfectness."*
(COLOSSIANS 3:14)

STORY

The Lord had really blessed Tammy and Sam. They were now on their way for him to coach in a bigger football conference and a much larger city. Though she knew things would also be challenging in a different environment, she thought it would be much better than last time.

The new journey offered great incentives and a substantial pay of more than $100k. Now, she was not the youngest wife on the staff. There was a woman named Lisa who was newly married, and her husband was the graduate assistant. They did not make a lot of money, and Tammy knew how that felt. Lisa shared that she was struggling in her marriage and that she was not able to enjoy the life of being a coach's wife.

Tammy asked Lisa if she could pray for her. They prayed and Tammy felt led to help financially and be a mentor to Lisa. Tammy had a mentor back in Utah. When she asked Lisa, Lisa was hesitant. Tammy believed God blessed her so that she could be a blessing to someone else. She only hoped Lisa would accept her help.

APPLICATION

When you are rewarded with the desires of your heart, it does not mean that everything is going to play out the way you want it. When you remove yourself out of the situation and allow God to do His due diligence, you will not be disappointed. You just have to accept His goodness, sit back and watch the transformation occur before your eyes.

You may not feel that you are deserving of the blessings that have come your way. However, it is key that you let the negatives go and embrace the positives. You must learn to accept that His grace is sufficient above all and always walk with great faith.

PRAYER

Father, I come to You thanking You for all the many blessings You have given. Though I have doubted You and questioned You, You still continue to shower me with Your blessings. You have blessed me through all my shortcomings and made me a true believer. Father, I know I will continue to make mistakes, but I will never forget the God I serve. You sit high and You look low in every situation that comes my way, and I thank You for seeing in me what I cannot see. Amen.

DAY 5

MERCY AND NO LOVE

Are you showing love the way God loves you?

"Charity suffereth long, and is kind; charity envieth not; charity vaunteth not itself, i s not puffed up, Doth not behave itself unseemly, seeketh not her own, is not easily provoked, thinketh no evil."

(*I CORINTHIANS 13:4-5*)

STORY

A few years later, Lisa's husband got a job in the top football conference. His salary had surpassed Tammy's husband. Though Tammy was elated for Lisa, but she felt some type of way about the fact that her husband was not receiving the higher salary. She felt like her

husband deserved to be a coordinator or a head coach. Afterall, he had put in more time. He was winning, and the NFL was drafting his players.

Tammy was becoming bitter knowing that black coaches just were not getting as much love and opportunity as others. When Sam became disappointed and lost his love for football, Tammy knew she could not stay angry. She began reading the Word and growing stronger spiritually. She began sharing life lessons with Sam. While they felt things were not always fair, they knew God was in control and loved them. Would that be enough?

APPLICATION

On this journey we call life, there are going to be times that you will be knocked down. The key is not to stay down, but to get back up. Not everything in life will come easy. It is a constant fight that comes with a lot of praying. Most of all, you must remember who you are and whose you are. You must learn to love your neighbors, your enemies, and the strangers you encounter the same way that God loves you. Remember, there will be those who do not want to see you succeed, but that is not your battle to fight.

When you put God first and allow Him to manifest in your life, you cannot lose, regardless of who is plotting against you. Always allow Him to use you so that you can sow a seed into the lost. Let them know that God is real. If He did it for you, He can do the same for them. You can help others catch that same flame you have for God!

PRAYER

Father, I thank You for blessing and keeping me covered through this journey. Father, I know that without You there is no me. Father, I know there have been times when I got so wrapped up with my daily and worldly life that I forgot to give You the quality time that you so deserve. Lord Jesus, help me to continue to be a beacon of light so that I can continue to speak Your Word to lost souls. Father, I ask and pray that You will continue to give me the courage and voice to speak Your truth always. Father God, You are worthy and I give You all the praise. In Jesus' name, Amen.

DECEMBER
WEEK 3

DAY 1
UNDERSTANDING LISTENING

Do you know what it means to listen?

*"Wherefore, my beloved brethren,
let every man be swift to hear, slow to speak,
slow to wrath." (*
JAMES 1:19)

STORY

Imani and Michelle have been best friends since elementary school; they are as close as sisters. They have been admitted to their dream college and are excited about everything that lies ahead. Naturally, they decide to room together, and they quickly learn that they need to listen to each other if they ever want to work through their conflicts.

Imani is the first to arrive home one day, and when Michelle gets there, she is very angry that the sink is full of dishes. Imani dirtied most of them. Michelle immediately rips into to Imani, yelling, "You *always* do this! You *never* clean up after yourself! Why is that? How hard could that possibly be?!"

Imani is very calm and tells her that she will leave the room for a few moments to give Michelle time to cool off. When she returns, Imani tells Michelle to sit down on the sofa so that they can talk. She explains to Michelle that, while she has valid concerns about the kitchen, she and Imani had a serious discussion recently about personal matters Imani was dealing with that were affecting her overall well-being. Imani reminds Michelle that she also told her that she would need some flexibility with household tasks.

Michelle suddenly remembers the conversation and admits to Imani that she heard her when they were talking. However, she did not really listen because she was preparing for a big exam at the time and was not focused. Michelle then profusely apologizes and asks for forgiveness. Imani accepts the apology and explains to Michelle that she left the room in the middle of her tirade because she did not want to become angry and say something that she would later regret. She knew that the most appropriate and effective response was to not say anything in the heat of the moment and to avoid becoming angry about the situation. While she did have the right to have those feelings, it was best not to say anything because it would only aggravate the situation and not resolve the conflict. The women now have a mutual agreement to truly listen to each other, address their concerns when they arise, and avoid speaking out in anger.

APPLICATION

Sometimes, it can be hard to bite your tongue when you think an argument is about to start or even if you are in the middle of one. The other person is probably saying something that is hurtful, untrue, or unfair, and your first instinct is lash out. That might feel good in the moment, but you will probably feel badly afterwards. You might say something that you cannot take back and ruin a relationship that is important to you.

The book of James provides Christians with a guide for how we should conduct ourselves in different situations. It advises us to place greater weight and value on hearing rather than speaking. Not doing this can lead to unfortunate outcomes. Taking this approach also helps us to let our thoughts calm down so that we can think clearly and have a levelheaded response to situations. More importantly, this helps us to be more like Jesus, even though it might be hard.

Take a few minutes to write down topics or issues that might trigger negative feelings within you. What do you think is at the root of those feelings? Why might you have such a response? How do you typically manage those reactions and emotions? Having emotions and feelings is valid, but you have to learn how to manage them; otherwise, you might create more problems than you already had.

The Bible says that God renews our minds daily, and He can surely do that when it comes to how we interact with other people and respond to things that they might say or do that we do not like or agree with for whatever reason. If this is an area where you need help, then pray daily and ask God to guide your tongue, mind, and heart so that you will be in the right frame of mind (and heart) when these situations arise.

PRAYER

Dear Lord, please help me to be a better listener. I am human and have a range of emotions. It is my earnest prayer that You guide me so that I only have emotions, thoughts, and ways that are like You. Please help me to be more like You and not let my flesh get the best of me. I want to be the best person I can be to my family, friends, and colleagues. That means that I need to learn how to listen better so that I can be a good communicator. More importantly, help me to listen so that I can be wiser and have healthier relationships. Help me to understand that my emotions are normal, but there is a time and a place to express them. Above all, help me to be more like You every day. Amen.

DAY 2
ACCEPTING INSTRUCTION

Are you ever too "grown" to receive instruction?

"Hear counsel, and receive instruction,
that thou mayest be wise in thy latter end."
(PROVERBS 19:20)

STORY

Imani is applying for her first real job as a recent college graduate, and several companies make her offers. One of the offers carries a substantial salary for a young person. Another pays less but can potentially lead to great professional opportunities. The last offer is one with average pay that would be a decent stepping-stone until something better comes along.

Imani decides to talk to her mother and seek advice about what she should do. During their conversation, her mother shares that she believes it would be wisest for Imani to take the job that it is more aligned with her career goals, whereas the other two would not make her happy and may derail her.

"Mom, what about the money, though? If I take the higher salary, I will have a lot of cash to save for vacations and to help you and Dad. I know you don't need it, but I am to give back to you," says Imani.

Her mother responds, "Imani, trust me. You will be better off with the other job. While the money sounds good, you will not be happy with either of those other two jobs."

Imani then says, "Well, in the end, it's my decision."

Imani makes her decision and accepts the higher paying job. After two months of working there, she goes to her mother and tells her that she should have heeded her advice and taken the other job. She is unhappy and is fully aware of the fact that she has no opportunities for upward mobility. Imani also said, "I really should have listened because you were right. You have experiences that I took for granted. I did not think you understood or could relate to what I was facing. I appreciate your wisdom, and thank you for loving me."

Imani now has wisdom about career goals and decision-making in an area of her life that is very new to her. She is also recognizing the importance of heeding the advice of others. They have wisdom that can be beneficial if she just prays and asks God for guidance in making the best decision that will help her reach her destiny.

APPLICATION

Life decisions sometimes require that we seek guidance and counsel from other people who have wisdom and experience that we do not. That is not always the easiest thing to do, especially when we rely on ourselves to do what we think is best or follow our guts.

It is not a requirement that we get advice from family or friends when making those important decisions; however, we can sometimes benefit from consulting with a parent, friend, or someone close to us whom we trust and respect. When facing important decisions, try going to a believer who has similar experiences and will give you their honest opinion. More importantly, because they are Christian, God might be speaking to you through them so that you know He is all-powerful and imparts wisdom and knowledge to us by way of a wise and trusted loved one.

PRAYER

Lord, I ask that You use whomever, whenever, and however to speak to me so that I know I am in Your will. I know that situations will come where I cannot make decisions on my own because I might be afraid and just do not know what to do. There will also be times when I will know or think that I know what I should do. Whatever the case may be, I ask that You crown my head with wisdom, knowledge, and understanding so that I can do what You have called me to do. No decision is too big or too small. I thank You in advance for Your guidance and protection. Amen.

DAY 3
FAITHFUL HEARING

Are you ready for what you might hear?

*"So then faith cometh by hearing,
and hearing by the word of God."*
(ROMANS 10:17)

STORY

Imani was faced with what she believed was one of the biggest decisions of her life. She had given her all to her current employer, but she was at a crossroads. Imani was no longer happy because she felt taken for granted. She had accumulated many accolades over the past three years, but she had reached her limits.

Imani finally fervently prayed to God and asked Him to take control of the situation. This was a faith walk like none other. She knew that she needed God to move mountains, and she chose to lean completely on Him. Imani's family members noticed a calm over her, and they could not understand why. This was uncharacteristic because Imani was usually always stressed and worried.

Two months later, Imani received an invitation to apply for a dream job she never knew she wanted. After careful prayer, she accepted the invitation, and soon she had the interview. She continued to pray throughout the process to make sure this was of God. At every turn, He confirmed His plans for her, which gave her tremendous peace. The company eventually extended the offer to her, and she was ecstatic. It was not until then that she told her family.

Imani's mother Ahmad warned her not to be hasty, while her father made a list of things he believed she should negotiate. Her parents meant well, but Imani did her homework and was aware of what was normal and appropriate to request as part of her package. She had a month to negotiate and receive her contract, so she used that time to pray and seek God, which involved avoiding conversations with other people so that she could make sure she was making the right decision.

The final offer made from the company was staggering, above and beyond everything Imani could ever ask or think. God awarded her obedience and built up her faith as she was still and quiet during this process. This was a great testament of faith to her family and friends because they saw Imani move in faith as she sought God for direction. Her experience encouraged them to be quiet, hear God, and wait on Him to fulfill His good and perfect will in their lives.

APPLICATION

In order to have faith, we must have blind, unwavering confidence in God. This also requires that we take a posture that allows us to listen and hear what He is telling us. He can speak to us through His Word or people. We have to be in a place where we are willing to hear what He says to us. God promises to take care of every need we have and to be with us always. He also wants us to have faith, and that requires us to trust in Him no matter how things look.

What do you trust God to do in your life? Where is your faith? Do you know how to listen to Him? You can grow your faith and trust in God by reserving quiet time for just the two of you, almost like you are on a date. Spend regular time in His Word and just talking to Him. You will notice that He will speak to you in those still, quiet moments, just when you need Him most.

PRAYER

Dear Lord, I ask that you teach me how to hear from You and listen to Your voice. I know that I will make mistakes because I am human, but I am also Your child. I am trusting You with my whole heart to speak to me and guide me in all that You would have me to do. I will purpose to be still, seek Your voice, and search my heart to know that I am in Your good and perfect will. Amen.

DAY 4
PRACTICING SILENCE

*What might people think of you
if you remain silent?*

*"Even a fool, when he holdeth his peace,
is counted wise: and he that shutteth his lips
is esteemed a man of understanding."*
(PROVERBS 17:28)

STORY

Having been at her new job for a couple of months, Imani really enjoys the company and her position. She gets along with everyone and makes it a point to soak in as much as she can. She observes the organizational culture and speaks up primarily when she feels an urgency to do so. While she does contribute to team

59

discussions and at other meetings, she is mindful of when she chooses to speak or to remain silent.

Imani has a coworker named Sally who is the complete opposite of her. Sally is always very quick to tell everyone about the many problems at the company that she sees needing to be addressed and fixed. In some instances, she is right and higher-ups actually investigated and found that some of her claims were valid. Because she is *always* voicing her concerns to anybody and everybody who will listen, Sally is beginning to lose the respect of her colleagues and bosses. Imani is personally concerned because the woman is not always right, and when Sally talks to her, Imani feels uncomfortable due to the strife and contention the woman seems to be sowing.

One day, Imani and Sally are in the break room at the same time, which Imani immediately dreads. Sally tells her, "I have been here for a long time, and I know the ins and outs. You know the saying, 'The squeaky wheel gets the oil,' right? Well, you need to be the squeaky wheel if you want to make it here. Trust me."

Imani politely thanks her for the advice and returns to her office. While she respects Sally as a person, she believes it is unwise to heed this advice. Instead, she continues to remain quiet for the most part, mainly because she is still learning the organization and is only speaking up when she feels it is appropriate.

This decision has resulted in Imani's colleagues having a considerable amount of respect and admiration for her. They see that she is hard working and wise, which also tells them that she will stand up for herself when necessary. They also know that she is somewhat of a moral compass for her team and the company. While it is Imani's personality to remain quiet for the most part, she also recognizes the importance of speaking up when necessary.

APPLICATION

Has there ever been a time when you had to "bite your tongue"? It might have been hard to do, but you realized that the benefit of doing so was so much more important than speaking in that moment. It might be difficult to hold back, but the bigger lesson here is that we must all use wisdom about when we should speak up or remain silent. Neither is a bad thing.

Speaking up does not always mean strength, and being silent is not a sign of weakness. Both can be positive or negative attributes depending on when and how they are used. That makes it even more important to pray so that you are behaving in ways that align with what God would have you to do.

PRAYER

Dear Lord, please give me wisdom about when to speak and when to remain silent. I want to bring glory and honor to Your name in all that I do, and that means that I must be obedient to whatever You are instructing me to say or do. I call my flesh under subjection so that I can move myself out of the way so that Your Holy Spirit can rest, rule, reign, and abide in me. I thank You for guiding my tongue and teaching me that being silent can be a wise thing that works for my good. Thank You in advance for Your guidance and instruction. Amen.

DAY 5
USING WISDOM

*How do you know when to speak up
and when to be silent?*

*"The LORD shall fight for you,
and ye shall hold your peace."*
(EXODUS 14:14)

STORY

Imani works part-time as a university professor. She loves teaching and watching her undergraduate and graduate students get excited about the different diversity issues she addresses in each of their class meetings. Although those conversations are oftentimes difficult, she is committed to addressing these issues in her classroom. After all, she has helped groom the

next generation of business professionals for fifteen years and knows that this is her calling.

A seminar becomes intense when a graduate student asks about the role of Christianity in how people from diverse backgrounds are mistreated, even discriminated against. Imani does her best to explain this in a very honest and forthcoming way. After much class discussion, the woman has a better understanding of the issue and appreciates the honest dialogue they have had.

A few weeks go by, and Imani learns that a student has falsely reported her class interactions with students to other faculty. This is troubling for her because the report was inaccurate. It was blatantly false! Imani is also informed that her colleagues have conducted an informal investigation into her treatment of students from a particular background.

This was such a stressful time for Imani, but God was her strength. How could her colleagues believe such lies? Why didn't they trust her? How on earth could this have happened? In the midst of everything, she was suddenly reminded of a prophetic word she received nearly a year prior where God sent a warning yet comforting word. God warned her of the specifics of this situation but assured her that she was going to be surrounded by soldiers who would lift her up. He promised her victory.

While Imani was initially afraid of what was going on, she finally found peace and comfort in the belief that she was going to get through this. She became leery of her colleagues, rightfully so, and even more trusting of God as to her protector and provider. The investigation eventually yielded nothing.

In fact, Imani was held in even higher esteem because the students only had positive things to say about her as a professor and mentor.

APPLICATION

When we are in a battle, it is hard not to take matters into our own hands. We naturally think that we can fix it, but if we are not careful, we can actually do more harm than good. That is why it is so important to pray without ceasing and to seek God fervently when these tests and trials come. We do not always know why they come to us, but we can rest assured that God will fight our battles for us. By trusting in Him, we are growing our faith in Him and allowing Him to show us who He is for us in a very personal way. During those times, it is very important that we remain silent and let God do all of the fighting and talking for us.

PRAYER

Dear Lord, I thank You for being Abba Father. You are everything to me. I entrust everything in my life to You because I know that You love me, will take care of everything that concerns me, and will fight the enemy on my behalf. I pray that You give me peace in all things, no matter what they look like. I praise You in advance for loving me in spite of myself. Thank You for Your divine covering and protection. Amen.

DECEMBER
WEEK 4

DAY 1
THE BLUEPRINT

What do you want?

*"And they said unto him, Ask counsel,
we pray thee, of God, that we may know whether our way
which we go shall be prosperous.
And the priest said unto them,
Go in peace: before the LORD is your way wherein ye go."*
(JUDGES 18:5-6)

STORY

Ugh! There are literally like ONE THOUSAND options to choose from, Kylie. How am I supposed to ever land on one?" Karrington hollered as she attempted to get her sister's sympathy while she frantically scrolled through her college course catalogue on her iPad trying to decide on her major. She was behind because it was already July, and classes would begin in late August!

Kylie, Karrington's older sister by 22.8 seconds, had her 3-5-7-10 year blueprint for success calculated and written down since her first year of college. Karrington, the free spirit, did not. She always relied on the phrase, "God's got me!"

The pressure was on since the twins would be entering their first semester of their junior year this fall. The golden rule was that by the junior year, students must solidify both their major and their specific concentration in order to graduate on time.

As usual, Kylie stepped out of her room into their living room to embrace her sister with a tight hug. "Kari, breathe. We are 20 years old, and you still freak yourself out over deciding what you want in life! Why?"

After taking a well-needed meditation break with her sister and a quick FaceTime call with their mother, Karrington was able to return to her search with a clear mind. Kylie and Karrington are each other's Yin and Yang. Their mother always told them that they were the perfect set of twins because they balance each other out.

"Mom always knows what to say!" Karrington cheerfully shared with Kylie, as she shoved her grouped list of potential careers towards her sister. "She had me pray, and then write out all of the potential careers I could envision myself in, group them together if there were similarities, and then link the majors and concentrations to each group!"

Following her mother's suggestion, Karrington determined her major for the fall.

APPLICATION

Define your expectation. Having to choose the right next step in life is not an easy task at all. We are reminded daily of the will that God gave us to choose our own path in life, but there is always a sense of calmness that should come when reflecting on how to layout our blueprint. He gives us an enormous amount of grace, and we must show ourselves the same amount of grace to know that sometimes we will not always make the right decision.

That is OKAY!

Take time to reflect on major life decisions that you have had to make in the past and remind yourself of how you prepared for them. Did you write them out or talk them out with God? If any process in the past did not include Him, this must change going forward. Remember that He expects us to have grand dreams, and larger than life aspirations for ourselves, knowing that we cannot do it on our own. God expects us to bring Him in at phase one, the planning phase, so that He may guide and light the steps of our journey ahead.

PRAYER

Dear God, I am not quite sure where, what, how, or when I want to move, but I know that if I come to You during my planning phase that You will cover me along the way with Your blood. I pray that You allow me to have a clear mind when sitting down to lay out my plan and that You never leave my side. Please give me the wisdom to make the right decisions when the time comes, but only if it's in Your will, God! I thank You in advance for all that is to come, and I love You, always. Amen.

DAY 2

THE CHALLANGE

How do we get there?

*"Trust in the LORD with all thine heart;
and lean not unto thine own understanding.
In all thy ways acknowledge him,
and he shall direct thy paths."*

(PROVERBS 3:5-6)

STORY

Kylie was the scientist and bookworm type while Karrington was the public relations and writer type. The one thing that Kylie loved about her sister was her ability to dream big, boisterous dreams. It was almost night and day when it came to how differently the two sisters viewed life.

"I think I'm going to head up to New York City this weekend Ky, do you want to come with?!" Karrington would frequently holler across their 1000 sq. foot apartment. Knowing exactly how much allowance their mother gave them monthly and how many packages had been showing up at the apartment, Kylie knew that if she agreed to tag along, Karrington would ask, "Can you cover the Megabus ticket for both of us, please?"

With aspirations to become the next black Carrie Bradshaw, Karrington was constantly trying to find ways to get to the city. It was a few days before New York Fashion Week would commence when she brought up the conversation again.

"Ya know Ky, if you come with me, Mom will be less upset that we left campus again to go to the city. Plus, you know me being in the mix will only help me get closer to achieving my dreams!"

Karrington loved pleading with her sister and concluding that it would be a step in the right direction to accomplishing her goals.

"Fine, Fine!" Kylie sighed as she gave in once again.

Her "yes" was followed by a tight hug, kiss on the cheek, and the words "I thank the heavens above for you!" Karrington always said this when Kylie folded.

Hook, line, and sinker … almost!

During the entire ride to the city, in typical Kylie fashion, she bombarded Karrington with a million and one questions to help her begin to lay the pieces of the puzzle together for her life goals. She suggested to Karrington that she go back to their mom's method of praying and then writing everything down because that was what helped her layout her mini goals to get to the larger goal: applying to medical school.

As Kylie poked at the empty gaps in Karrington's plan, it became even more clear that her sister would be in way over her head if she didn't break her grandiose goal into manageable bite sized pieces and if she didn't begin writing everything down.

APPLICATION

Laying out your path to success can seem like emptying out a 1000-piece puzzle onto the living room floor and not knowing where to begin. Luckily, there is always the picture on the puzzle box that we can use as our guide. The best way to attack the completion of a 1000-piece puzzle is to group all of the alike colors, shapes and anything else that remotely looks like it belongs together into a pile. This act of sorting and sifting is what we must do with the multitude of different ideas that we have in our heads as we are trying to choose whether to go left or right on our journey of life.

God encourages us to trust Him when it comes to guiding our footsteps and to trust to Him even if our path becomes blurry with fog. The same way we have the puzzle box picture as a reference point to reflect on the final picture, we must remember that God has the final picture of not just our goals that we are trying to accomplish but the entire picture of our lives. We must always lean towards Him for guidance, as He has promised that He already has our bigger picture mapped out, down to our anticipated next move. Do not get weary, but rest, and do not stress about the journey!

PRAYER

God, I am lost. I am leaning into Your guidance and not my own as I try to understand what my next move should be. Thank You for planting the seed of the journey in my life, and I will continue to praise You in advance for the blessings that are to come. I pray that in my times of frustration and confusion that You allow me to remain calm, cool, and collected. I remember that all Your promises are "Yes" and "Amen." Everything can come to fruition in Your name. You know my full masterpiece, and I am able to rest in knowing that I have cast all my cares and worries in Your hands, and now I no longer have doubt. I love You, always. Amen.

DAY 3
THE WAIT

Are we there yet?

*"Rest in the LORD, and wait patiently for him:
fret not thyself because of him who prospereth
in his way, because of the man who bringeth
wicked devices to pass."*

(PSALMS 37:7)

STORY

Winter break is the halfway mark in the school year where juniors in college tend to hit the "senior slip." Even though they have an entire semester plus another additional full year of school to complete before walking across the stage with their diploma, they tend to lose focus.

The first semester of their junior year was different from all prior semesters for the twins. Kylie was having a difficult time getting through her organic chemistry class, which was known as the hardest class within her undergraduate program. Kylie had been focused the twin her entire life. Karrington offering advice to her on how to cope while in the midst of the storm was something new.

"Ah! I cannot take this anymore. I might just have to take the loss," Kylie blurted out as she banged her hand against their kitchen table. Karrington jumped up from her Netflix-and-chill date to see what was going on with her sister. It was odd for her to see Kylie stressed out over anything, especially schoolwork.

"Ky, you've got this. Do you remember how you and mom always give me the look when I am frustrated? Now I am giving it to you. Breathe. Let's pray over it," Karrington said as she peeled the iPad from Kylies' grip and began to pray over her.

Karrington reminded Kylie that if she moved too fast, she would not get the chance to smell the flowers. She encouraged her to slow down sometimes. "If you are constantly running at a mile a minute, you may miss out on certain lessons that God is trying to teach you, Ky. You do not always have to be in a rush. It is in stillness where we get to see, hear, and experience God!"

APPLICATION

Growing pains are difficult. Waiting is hard because we are not God. Therefore, we have absolutely no way of knowing if we are still at the beginning, middle or end of a situation. We know that we have done enough to kick the can somewhat down the alley, but how far was our kick really? Two inches or two miles?

The bigger the goal, the longer the journey may seem. Remember that it is, indeed, okay to rest, especially when we feel like we are in the middle of our journey. Just like any athlete, no one can play a full game with 100% energy without stopping to hydrate and re-energize himself or herself.

Through it all, remember that you do not walk alone. God is always with you even in the middle of the storm.

P R A Y E R

God, I am anxious, but I know that when I come to You in this state, You will provide me peace. I ask that You take over my negative thoughts and replace them with positive affirmations and confirmations. I thank You for providing a filter in my mind that reassures me of where I am on my journey. You are the one that can make a way out of no way. Even if I am unable to know where I am specifically on my journey, I rest in knowing that You will never let Your children stray. I love You, always, Amen.

DAY 4
THE UNEXPECTED

How do you combat the unexpected?

*"And the LORD said unto him,
Wherewith? And he said, I will go forth,
and I will be a lying spirit in the mouth
of all his prophets. And he said, Thou shalt persuade him,
and prevail also: go forth, and do so."*

(I KINGS 22:22)

STORY

Kylie came out of the bathroom, and fell into her sister's arms sobbing, "Kari, what am I going to tell Mom? I'm pregnant."

Neither Kylie nor Karrington expected this to happen before both of them crossed the commencement stage in the spring. In their last two years of college, their roles had reversed when it came to nurturing. Now Karrington had to be the one to ease her sister's pain and let her know that despite this surprise, she would be okay.

"You know what the funny thing about this is, Ky?" Karrington asked as she sat on the floor holding Kylie in her arms.

"Nothing is funny right now," Kylie snarled back at her sister.

"Okay, maybe funny was not the right word. You are acting as if your world is ending when, in reality, it is just beginning. Trust in God with <u>all</u> your heart. Besides, for all we know, this could have been a part of your plan all along! We will figure this all out with guidance from God. Trust me and Him," she whispered in Kylie's ear as she pulled her in tightly and rocked her to sleep.

APPLICATION

Consider your roadblocks as blessings. Without roadblocks in life, we would not need to depend on God to help us maneuver through them. When God created us, He wanted us to be able to rely on Him for any and everything. He wants to be your source of light, love, peace and happiness. Allow Him to be that for you!

Be both agile and flexible when you come to this part in your journey. Sometimes, it does not matter if you did all the right things in life. With higher elevation comes higher devils and distractions that will try to pull your attention away from God. This is that exact time when you should come to Him more than ever before.

Even if there appears to be hiccups, there are never any missteps in the journey that He has created for us. Remember that we always have to make room to invite Him into our hearts.

PRAYER

Dear God, I am confused. I am lost. What are You trying to teach me in this moment of uncertainty and confusion? I pray that You open up my mind and heart to receive the lesson that You want to teach me. Just as children turn to their parents for answers, I am coming to You empty and ready for you to fill me up with your over abundant love and support while I am in the midst of the unexpected. I thank You in advance for the clarity that You will provide. I love you, always, Amen.

DAY 5
THE FINALE

What is the next step?

"For I know the thoughts that I think toward you, saith the LORD, thoughts of peace, and not of evil, to give you an expected end."
(JEREMIAH 29:11)

STORY

Kylie had everything planned out. Her 3-5-7-10 year plan was all set. She had planned on studying for the MCAT during her senior year of college and then heading straight into medical school after graduation. She did not plan to take any breaks.

"Pass me Princeton's bottle, please. He will not stop with the hungry tears Ky," Karrington hollered across the apartment.

The twins were living their postgraduate lives with new baby Princeton. Was he included within Kylie's 3-5-7-10 year plan? Yes, of course, but not within the first three years after undergraduate studies. She had planned for him to arrive much later.

As Karrington had promised Kylie, everything worked itself out as long as they were alignment with God. No matter what came their way, they always knew that no weapon formed against them would prosper. Karrington loved to remind Kylie, "Momma always likes to harp on *'They never said the weapon would not form... God just promised us that it would not harm us.'*"

"I know you may think that you were not prepared for this moment, Ky," Karrington began with Princeton on her hip, "but believe it or not, you have always had the soft skills to become a wonderful and nurturing mother. Anything you lack, He will provide for you!"

Kylie began to wipe a few tears from her face; it had been a while since the twins had one of their infamous heart to heart conversations.

"How will I get to my purpose now Kari?" Kylie questioned her sister.

"Ky, do not make me breakout into my gospel medley that mom used to play nonstop," Karrington joked. "You will become the doctor that you are destined to be Kylie, but in HIS time. I think that all this time you have been trying to live according to the plan you have written for yourself and not the plan that God has for you. Just have faith and know that He has prepared you for every blessing that is getting ready to come your way."

Karrington reminded her sister that all her good days outweighed her bad days. She reiterated that God's promises are of peace and not evil!

APPLICATION

The unknown is scary, but even scarier is trying to live a life according to our own idea of what the next steps should be. We risk ignoring God because we want our plan to be THE plan. Sometimes, we have to be okay with putting our plan to the side and being open to alternatives, trusting that at the end of that journey, we will still end up where we have prayed to be.

Figuring out your purpose is not an easy task either. Have you ever completed a project that you have been working on for a while, and even though it is finished, it still feels incomplete? That is what happens when we go through life with the intention of just checking the box. Push yourself to go beyond checking the box when trying to level up by pushing yourself out of your comfort zone and allowing God's will to be done, and not yours. Giving Him permission to have His way in your life will not be easy or comfortable, but it will be rewarding.

PRAYER

Dear God, what is next? As I journey into my next blessing, I want to thank You in advance for covering me in Your blood. When I show up, I want people to see You first. I continue to ask for whatever is in Your will for my life to flourish. Do not allow any worldly desires to block that blessing. Provide me with both patience and discernment to know what is for me at the right time. I also ask that I be willing to wait for the right thing and not what may be convenient in the moment. I love you, always, Amen.

DECEMBER
WEEK 5

DAY 1
JESUS CARES
Does it really matter?

*"When Jesus therefore saw his mother,
and the disciple standing by, whom he loved,
he saith unto his mother, Woman, behold thy son!
Then saith he to the disciple, Behold thy mother!
And from that hour that disciple took her
unto his own home."*
(JOHN 19:26-27)

STORY

W hy should I attend? They only want you. They will never accept me, but they all like you. I'm only being invited because they know that you and I are close friends," Ginger stated wearily.

Ginger suffered from low self-esteem. She never believed that she was good enough, smart enough, or pretty enough. Her friend Amber always tried to increase Ginger's confidence, but rarely did Ginger believe anything positive that was said about her.

"That is not true, and you know it. You just do not see yourself the way others see you. You are one of the kindest, most giving women I know. People enjoy being around you. They love you and they love your spirit. You just will not allow yourself to enjoy being you and being in the company of others who enjoy you," Amber responded.

"Ginger, perhaps this is all the result of something in your past that has not yet been resolved. Who knows? What I do know is that you matter. Your life, your work, and your dreams all matter," Amber stated as she gently took her closest friend by the hand. "You have got to stop counting yourself out. I wonder how many great opportunities you have missed out on because you do not feel worthy or accepted."

Feeling a little less fearful, Ginger began to relax. She wanted so badly to believe the things that Amber and others said about her. In that moment, she realized that her self-esteem needed a boost. However, she knew that she could not accomplish this alone.

Amber offered, "Let's do this together. Let's attend the meeting to see what the organization has to offer. Who knows? It may not be a fit for my goals and my passion, but I will never know unless I go."

APPLICATION

Have you ever felt like you just did not fit in anywhere? Do you always compare yourself to others, afraid of not being good enough? Sometimes, we are our own worst enemy and our biggest critic. If we could only see ourselves the way God sees us and believe how much he loves us, our lives would be so much better.

The Bible teaches us that we are fearfully and wonderfully made, but we easily forget this when we are feeling inadequate and left out. To assure us of this fact, we have a gentle reminder of a compassionate Savior who cares for us at all times, wherever we are. There is no measure, standard, or rank that we must garner to win Him over to our side. He is already there with us always.

PRAYER

Lord Jesus, thank You for caring for me when I am feeling alone and unwanted. Help me to see myself the way that You see me and to know that I matter. Thank You for never leaving me and always providing for me. Please change my thoughts about myself and teach me how to value myself, knowing that even in my faults, You, Lord, still care. In the name of Jesus, Amen.

DAY 2
JESUS HEALS

How can this be?

"But the woman fearing and trembling,
knowing what was done in her,
came and fell down before him,
and told him all the truth. And he said unto her,
Daughter, thy faith hath made thee whole;
go in peace, and be whole of thy plague."

(MARK 5:33-34)

STORY

The meeting went well. Ginger was excited because the organization's mission matched what she loved to do.

"But why do they want me to join? I really cannot believe that they value me the way they say they do. How can they possibly want me with all my

past mistakes? I have done things that have not made me proud. My life is far from perfect," Ginger yelled to Amber from an adjacent room.

Amber could not believe her ears. No one is perfect. Why couldn't Ginger just be thankful for the opportunity to apply for membership?

"Look Ginger, everybody has a past and has made mistakes along the way. Let's stay focused here! We have been invited to submit our application, and that is what we are going to do. We are not going to beat ourselves up with our past. I know you are in shock right now because you have doubted yourself for so long, but this is real. Let's do our part. Let's complete the application!" Amber yelled back as she walked into the garage, closing the door behind her.

Ginger realized that she doubted herself again. She wondered why she found it so difficult to recognize the good in her.

APPLICATION

Being invited to become a part of something larger than ourselves is amazing and beautiful at the same time. The problem comes when we begin to hold our lives up to the mirror of our past. It is there in the mirror that we lose our self-esteem. It is there, where we find the wounds that still leak. It is there where, we ponder too long on the would haves, should haves and could haves.

It is also right there where God steps in to heal the broken pieces of our lives. He knows us intimately and longs to heal us deeply. There is nothing too hard for God when we release it over to Him to handle.

PRAYER

Lord Jesus, today I bring You all the broken pieces of my past. I admit to You that I have done many wrongs in my past and pray that You forgive me for my actions and deeds. I ask You to help me receive Your healing balm in the places that I need it most. Help me to walk upright and know that You have healed me and that I should not be still carrying the weight of my past. In the name of Jesus, Amen.

DAY 3
JESUS RESTORES

Who is at fault?

*"When Jesus had lifted up himself,
and saw none but the woman, he said unto her,
Woman, where are those thine accusers?
hath no man condemned thee? She said, No man, Lord.
And Jesus said unto her, neither do I condemn thee:
go, and sin no more."*
(JOHN 8:10-11)

STORY

Pulling the door open, Ginger whispered, "But Amber, you do not understand. I was not always kind. When I was a teenager, I retaliated against someone who hurt me badly. I never apologized. I wanted them to hurt the way they hurt me. What if the membership committee found out? I don't know. I just do not want my life on display. I am going to leave this alone. I am not applying and that is final," she stated.

It was days before Ginger and Amber would be interviewed to determine whether they would be granted membership. Ginger had tossed and turned all night. She believed that she would have to answer questions about her past, and she did not want the members to know some of the ungodly acts she had committed.

"Girl you are something else," Amber said, shaking her head. "Are you seriously worried about something you did as a teenager? Is this why you have been so sheltered and reserved about engaging in community service? I do not believe this! You are thirty-two years old, and you are hanging your entire life on a mistake from fifteen years ago. Give it a rest already! Look at the application; it does not ask if you ever did anything you were not proud of."

Amber asked Ginger if the person that hurt her had apologized. "I bet they are living their best life, not thinking about you or what you did to them. You need to make peace with your past so you can get on to your real life and the future that awaits you," Amber encouraged.

Ginger gave what Amber said some serious thought. She decided to try to figure out how to get beyond her past.

APPLICATION

Misplaced guilt has the uncanny ability to hold us hostage. It often causes us to live in the shadows of our lives, peering around every corner for our past, hoping that it does not show up and consume our future.

This is not what the Bible means when it says that God has a plan for us. Jesus came to heal the sick, restore sight to blind, mend broken hearts and restore us. It is in this place of restoration that we find the sweet release of God's presence in our lives. This presence allows us the full expression of who we are in Jesus. He loves us too much to leave us like He found us. He lovingly restores us and sets us free.

PRAYER

Lord Jesus, thank You for not leaving me the way you found me. You are amazing, Lord! Thank You that even when You see my flaws and all, You restore me by taking the guilt of my past and removing it far from me. Help me to live freely in the fullness of Your presence. In the name of Jesus, Amen.

DAY 4
JESUS DELIVERS

What should you do?

"Ask, and it shall be given you; seek, and ye shall find;
knock, and it shall be opened unto you:
For every one that asketh receiveth;
and he that seeketh findeth;
and to him that knocketh it shall be opened."
(MATTHEW 7:7-8)

STORY

Amber, I really do not know how to get beyond this," Ginger confessed. "I have wrestled with my actions for such a long time. Every time I think I am over it, the situation surfaces again in my mind. I must admit that I secretly follow the person on social media to see if she is okay. I am

often tempted to reach out to her to apologize, but I cannot face the possibility of rejection."

Ginger had become a social media stalker. As she scrolled through the posts made by her former classmate, she was somewhat jealous of how happy she appeared. It did not seem as if she had been impacted by Ginger's actions at all.

Come sit down, and let's talk through this," Amber said, as she pointed to a chair near her. "Ginger, you have got to give yourself some grace and receive forgiveness for your past. Why not send a message to her inbox and apologize? It she receives it, fine. If not, it is still fine.

Amber reminded Ginger of what she had accomplished, finishing graduate school at the top of her class; owning her home; always giving and donating to causes; and being kind to everybody. She encouraged her to get a therapist to help her deal with the situation.

APPLICATION

Our thoughts can sometimes get the best of us. We spend too much time thinking and not enough time doing. When it comes down to it, we struggle with our emotions and our thoughts so much that we convince ourselves that there can only be one possible outcome.

Praise God that Jesus is not limited in His ability to deliver us from ourselves. We find countless biblical examples of how He went about healing, restoring, and delivering people, even from themselves. Some only had to ask for what they needed from Him and He answered favorably. When we ask in His name, He delights in hearing from us, and He readily answers us.

PRAYER

Lord Jesus, You are the answer to every prayer. I come now asking You to take my thoughts captive. Lord, I am tired of wrestling with the same old thoughts. Please filter them through Your love, releasing back to me those things that are useful, purposeful and life giving. In the name of Jesus, Amen.

DAY 5

JESUS SAVES

Is it too late?

"And he said unto Jesus, Lord, remember me when thou comest into thy kingdom. And Jesus said unto him, Verily I say unto thee, Today shalt thou be with me in paradise."

(LUKE 23:42-43)

STORY

Do you really think it would work? After all, this happened so long ago. I just do not know if I can handle it if she is still angry," Ginger responded. "What if my actions stir up an old wound and cause her to feel bad or relive the situation?"

Ginger had almost convinced herself to reach out to the person she had hurt. Still, she was apprehensive about the response she would receive.

"Ginger, this has to be about your healing," Amber said. "It has to be about you being free from the pain of the past. How are you going to do that without going through the process? Stop trying to live in someone else's thoughts. Stop trying to figure out what her response will be and just do your part. Send the apology, then leave it alone. You can only control how you respond."

Amber encouraged Ginger to log on to social media and send the message without any expectation. She promised her friend that this simple act would help her forgive herself and release the stress that she had carried for so many years.

APPLICATION

Time is on your side. It is never too late to respond to the love of Jesus. When we come to Jesus from a place of truth, He hears us and responds to us, no matter the time.

It is never too late to ask for forgiveness. It is never too late to make a course correction. Jesus delights in change. He lived to reclaim us, and He died to save us.

PRAYER

Lord Jesus, thank You for making all things beautiful in Your time. Help me today, Lord, as I receive the forgiveness You have made available to me and extend the olive branch asking for forgiveness from those whom I offended. I believe this is the appointed time and that You have prepared me for this moment. In the name of Jesus, Amen.

JANUARY
WEEK 6

DAY 1
JOY IN THE VALLEY

What do you do when all of your joy is gone?

"Now the God of hope fill you with all joy and peace in believing, that ye may abound in hope, through the power of the Holy Ghost."
(ROMANS 15:13)

STORY

Eva found out her marriage was broken. She was grief-stricken. Proud of her family dynamics, she did not understand how to keep things from falling apart. Her season as a wife was ending, and she felt she would be raising her children solo.

Anna tried to encourage Eva, saying, "You are beautiful, smart, and thoughtful. You need to hold your head high and live your life without shame."

Eva was struggling. Her family was her life. She asked herself, "What do you do when all your joy is gone?"

Anna told Eva that everyone goes through heartbreak, but it is not healthy to stay there. When a chapter is closed, you have to rewrite your story. She encouraged her to continue to invest in her children, write the books she had put on hold, and establish her consulting firm. She told her, "Whatever you do, don't give up hope, and find joy in the simple things."

APPLICATION

No one wants to experience trials and tribulation. These cause an array of emotions. One of the most relatable emotions is pain.

Pain is an unpleasant feeling. It can take on many forms. It can be sharp, dull, stinging, and burning. Sometimes, life does not go as we planned. We must trust that God knows what it best and that He will lead us from good to better to best.

PRAYER

Dear Lord, the Word says that weeping may endure for a night, but joy comes in the morning. No one is exempt from pain and struggles. Help me find my joy. Fill me with joy, hope, and peace. Help me feel the power of Your Holy Spirt. Please guide my thoughts and help me realize the pain will push me to my purpose. Please order my steps towards complete healing. Amen.

JOY IN MY SOUL

How do I find joy?

*"Grant thee according to thine own heart,
and fulfil all thy counsel."*
(PSALM 20:4)

STORY

Anna recommended a weekend getaway for Eva. This would give her the opportunity regroup and think about some things. She knew Eva had a lot on her mind and was always placing everyone's needs before her own. She convinced Eva to visit a wellness community for a weekend, so she could connect to nature and to God.

Anna felt this was what Eva needed. The community had fresh food and fresh air. Focused on well-being, the community was set in the midst of acres of preserved forests and meadows with miles of nature trails connecting homes, restaurants, and businesses. It offered guests several amenities.

Eva had a lot on her mind, so she invested in herself and signed up for a yoga class. It was difficult for her to relax. When she closed her eyes, all her concerns flashed across her mind. The instructor informed her several times to breathe. At one point, she felt as though she would hyperventilate.

APPLICATION

Most of the time, we do not have all the answers, so we try to figure things out immediately without thinking or praying. Before a plane departs, the flight attendants explain what to do in case of an emergency. They inform you to mask yourself before helping others.

Often in life, we try to rush through phases. We must take time to breath. Effective breathing can not only provide you with a greater sense of mental clarity, but it can also help you sleep better, digest food more efficiently, improve your body's immune system, and reduce stress levels. We must understand that before we can help others, we must be well ourselves. It is ok to make yourself a priority.

PRAYER

Dear Lord, help me be more aware of my needs. Help me cultivate healthy habits. Help me to heal from the inside out and forgive me for not treating myself as I deserve to be treated. Each and every day, remind me to exhale because You know the plans You have for me. Please reveal them to me so that I can find authentic joy in my soul. Amen.

DAY 3

JOY IN MY SPIRIT

Father, can you hear me?

"Rejoicing in hope; patient in tribulation; continuing instant in prayer."
(ROMANS 12:12)

STORY

After the weekend at the wellness community, Anna encouraged Eva to consider professional counseling. Eva was offended because she thought Anna was inferring that she was unstable. Anna explained that, sometimes, it could be overwhelming to figure things out alone. Eva was still on the fence and did not understand why her friend did not have faith to believe that she could fix her own problems.

Anna shared that her therapist helped her identify goals and potential solutions to problems. She explained how counseling decreased her emotional turmoil. Eva could not imagine talking to a stranger about her personal business. Anna reminded her that her journey might empower someone else.

APPLICATION

We could all benefit from improving our communication and coping skills. These skills help strengthen self-esteem as well as promote behavior changes and optimal mental health. Mental health is just as important as physical health. So, give it all to God.

When you spend time with God, your spirit and mind are strengthened. You are happier. You are more loving. You are a better you. Therefore, make sure that you make time to give Him all the glory, honor and praise.

PRAYER

Lord, thank You for giving me an ear to listen. Help me to understand that when things are not going the way I would like, I must trust in You. Lord, help me to put my confidence in You. Thank You, Lord, for the professional helpers You have equipped to guide me through these turbulent times. Lord, I thank You that I am learning how to rejoice in your hope. Amen.

DAY 4
JOY IN MY HEART

What brings happiness to my life?

"A merry heart doeth good like a medicine:
but a broken spirit drieth the bones."
(PROVERBS 17:22)

STORY

Eva realized that she is in charge of her own happiness and joy, so she tried something different. She started her day out by reading a devotional book that Anna gave her. Eva was a little reluctant. At first, she made the argument that she did not have time. She quickly realized self-care is the best care. Eva shared with Anna that the more she began to read the devotional on daily basis, the better she felt. Eva began to feel a joy within that she had never experienced.

APPLICATION

Medicine makes us feel better when taken as instructed. Likewise, when our countenance changes from sad to glad, it gives us new energy, a fresh zeal, revival, and restoration. We can move forward rather than remaining in depression and gloom.

Life is about choices, and every action has consequences. Everything we say and do has consequences. Our actions have a ripple effect. Positive thoughts become positive actions.

PRAYER

Lord, thank You for a merry heart. Continue to cultivate my heart that I may experience Your joy in ways I never have before. Lord, continue to reveal, guide, and lead me to true happiness.

Lord, thank You for taking away the sadness, hopelessness, and loneliness. Lord, help me to share Your joy today. Amen.

DAY 5
JOY ALL OVER ME

How can I get joy back into my life?

*"Rejoice in the Lord always:
and again I say, Rejoice."*
(PHILIPPIANS 4:4)

STORY

Eva recognized that as she became more occupied with positive tasks and people, she began to feel better about the person she was becoming. She began to appreciate the sun shining, the flowers blooming, and the beautiful rainbow after the storm. Anna praised Eva for the glow she had. One morning, Eva looked at herself in the mirror and admitted, "I get it. I am one of God's beautiful creations. If He can make a closed flower bloom, He can certainly restore my joy."

Eva did not realize the impact she was having on others because of her joyful countenance. Yes, Eva was contagious because she allowed herself to become encapsulated with the joy of the Lord and all his creations.

APPLICATION

Practice, practice, practice. The more you do it, the more it becomes a part of you. Whether it is reading a daily devotional, speaking words of affirmation, praying, exercising or whatever makes you happy, do more of it.

Create good habits. Strong habits grow stronger over time and become more and more automatic. Make sure you have the right ones! Habits are powerful and create desire.

PRAYER

Lord, thank You for restoring my joy. Thank You, Lord, for giving me strength to endure the process. Lord, thank You for all the individuals who encouraged me and helped me along the way. Lord, thank You for drawing me closer to You and allowing me to have a meaningful relationship with You. Amen.

JANUARY
WEEK 7

DAY 1
FORGIVING THE UNAPOLOGETIC

Who should do the apologizing?

"And be ye kind one to another, tenderhearted, forgiving one another, even as God for Christ's sake hath forgiven you."
(EPHESIANS 4:32)

STORY

Faith woke up to a wonderful post from a friend who had a milestone birthday. It read, "I love everyone right now. I'm blessed to have shared this amazing ride with all those I've talked to, laughed with, cried with, hugged, argued with, celebrated with, walked away from, been left by, hurt, built up, cried over, loved, listened to your truth, received love from, broken bread with at your expense, learned from, refused to receive from, and respected! I have learned and grown from every one of these experiences. How can I be anything but grateful for that?"

These are the words of someone who has decided to commit to believing the biblical truth that all things work together for good for those who love God and are called according to His purpose.

Faith was instantly able to identify with the sentiments in her friend's post because life had not been so kind to her. On many occasions, she was left questioning God's presence and His very existence. When she decided not only to commit to attending church services, but to commit also to the study of God's Word and private worship, her understanding was increased, and her heart was opened to being healed and being completely restored.

Faith refused to put her life on hold any longer in hopes of receiving an apology she felt she was owed. She wanted her allegiance to be to God and not to holding a grudge or protecting herself behind of wall of pain and disappointment. She learned how to forgive others and to forgive herself by committing her ways to God.

APPLICATION

The Word of God clearly outlines that we are to go to our brother if we think we have offended and when we feel like we have been the offender. The responsibility of reconciliation is yours. However, you first need to be reconciled to God. Let Him lead you and soften your heart. It is important to love

God and understand His will for your life in order to endure and persevere.

Encounters of the worst kind inevitably work for Your good and not for your demise. As you continue this journey with Christ, keep in mind what belonging to the Kingdom affords you. Do not strive to look like a saint; live as one by keeping your covenant with the Father as He keeps His covenant with you! You are blessed! You are blessed!

P R A Y E R

Father God, I ask that You help me remain humble so that I can see my brothers and sisters in Christ as You see them. Help me not to be judgmental but to love unconditionally and pray for them diligently. Ultimately, I want to be more like You. Therefore, I ask that You help my unbelief and allow me to recognize Your love and patience towards me as I seek to forgive all who have offended me. Thank You for wrapping Your loving arms around me and caring for me when I do not care for myself. For this, I ask, in Jesus' name, Amen.

DAY 2

THINK LIKE CHRIST

Is Godly transformation what you need?

*"And be not conformed to this world;
but be ye transformed by the renewing of your mind,
that ye may prove what is that good,
and acceptable, and perfect, will of God."*

(ROMANS 12:2)

STORY

The way you think is truly a reflection of who you are. To look in the mirror with your spiritual eye and not like the reflection is cause for self-examination. Faith struggled for a long time with feelings of insecurity and not loving herself. She never thought she was good enough,

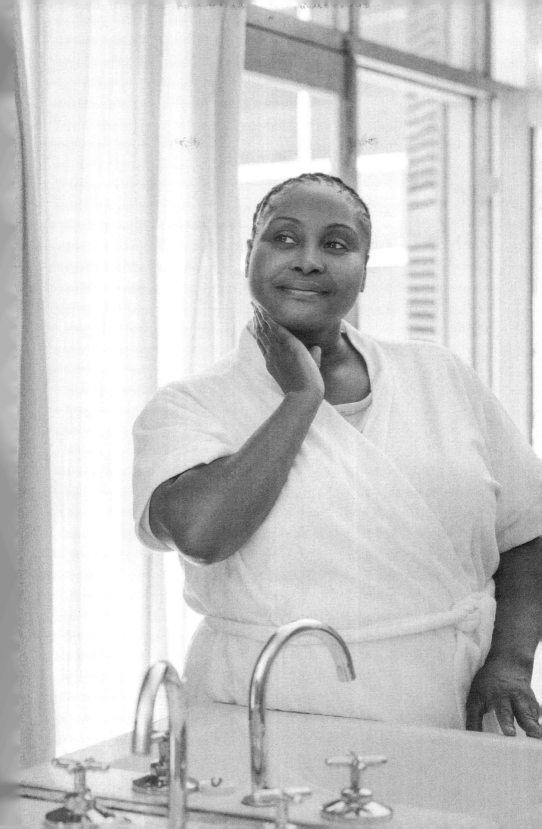

so she did what she thought would grant her acceptance in her desired friend group. When that did not satisfy her need, she sought after praise and attention wherever she found herself. Faith did not believe she was lovable; therefore, she was driven to fill this void.

Years later, she realized that her self-confidence was in the gutter. Not being who God called her to be took a toll on her thought process and her attitude. The need to perform to feel connected or approved became draining. With much resistance to the truth, initially, she began to wrestle with her demons. There was a commitment to change and a refusal to remain the same that became the turning point for redirecting the rest of her life for the better.

APPLICATION

Where there is no transformation, there is no growth! What you are facing may not make sense to you in the moment. However, consistently running your thoughts, feelings and reactions by God will bring about an understanding and divine peace to what may appear to be a painstakingly difficult situation. It would be advantageous to your growth if you ask yourself the following important questions:

Whom do I spend my time with? What do I spend my time doing? What do I enjoy doing most? How do I spend my money? Am I at peace with being alone with myself? Are the activities I engage in or people I engage with causing me to grow and evolve continuously in godliness? Am I comfortable enough in my skin to help build and encourage others in every situation?

If your responses are less than favorable, there is still hope. Love yourself enough to grapple with the truth of scriptures, and let God take the wheel. He will equip you to love unconditionally and walk in truth. He will also give you the strength to walk away from dysfunctional people and situations. When you know His will and walk in His plan, it makes the weight (people, possessions, and problems) of this world fall by the wayside. It all starts with a thought and a commitment to evolve!

PRAYER

Father God, I thank You for another day and the revelation of the importance of my need for transformation. Forgive me of my sins and cleanse me from all unrighteousness. Show me how to put on the mind of Christ concerning all things. As I continue through this day, let me be a light upon a hill for many to see Your good works and ask what they can do to be saved. Help me to remember that my life belongs to You and that my actions must represent You so that You may be glorified in the earth. Thank You for entrusting me to do a great work for You. In Jesus' name, I pray, Amen.

DAY 3
GOD BEARS ALL

*Do you have the spiritual stamina
to make it through this trial?*

*"Come unto Me, all ye that labour and are heavy laden,
and I will give you rest. Take my yoke upon you
and learn of me; for I am meek and lowly in heart;
and ye shall find rest unto your souls."*

(MATTHEW 11:28)

STORY

The Christmas decorations had been stored in their safe place. The sound of the holiday music had become a distant memory. The children were back to school, and work had resumed for many. Faith stood gazing of out the window, hoping to relive all the joy and excitement of the season, if just for one moment. Then life happened!

Faith went to the prayer line and discovered that a dear friend was in the midst of a natural disaster. There was one prayer petition after another requesting the strength to endure a fatal diagnosis, loss of employment, separation after death, divorce, and so on. All the residual holiday joy had been abruptly paralyzed by fear, hurt, and sadness.

Faith mustered up enough energy to get in her secret place and pour her heart out to God. After expressing her emotions, she had to find the strength and determination to stand. Faith felt the tug on her spirit to pray, but her body resisted the urge. Nevertheless, she found herself before God in prayer and song until she felt the weight lifted. Her warring in the spirit created peace for her as well as all those mentioned in her prayers.

APPLICATION

Sadness and pain may be the reality of many around you because storms in life are inevitable. When your family members, friends, or neighbors become affected by life's setbacks, you can feel the sting of anxiety and hopelessness as well. It is important to react appropriately when thoughts of giving up seem to be the only solution. You must commit to seeking God's face for strength and encouragement. God may not reveal His ultimate will in a situation, but He will respond to a broken spirit. God's promises will get you through.

There is strength and power in your ability to recall truth (the Word of God) and walk in it. When you understand your purpose and calling are for a cause larger than you, you can forge through despite the challenges of life. Finally, when you believe that God is forever present and able to provide relief and a place of refuge, you are empowered to love and serve with a smile.

God is there; He cares, and He wants to equip you with the tools you need to live victoriously! His strength is made known in your weakness. Activate your faith by laying it down at the His feet and resting in His presence. This will give you a renewed outlook on life and all that it brings. This truth is worth celebrating in all seasons!

PRAYER

Father God, I know You will not put on me more than I can bear. I want to thank You for that sound theology today. When I waiver in my faith, my heart is at peace knowing that You will undergird me. My trust is in You this day and forever more. Help me remain in a place to hear from You and be ready to respond to Your call. Help me to rejoice with those who rejoice and mourn with those who mourn. Give me eyes to see, ears to hear what the Spirit is doing and saying. My prayer is that I follow Your lead for Your glory. For these and many other blessings, I ask, in Jesus' name. Amen.

DAY 4
EMBRACE YOUR SEASON

Are you in position to flow with the move of God?

*"To everything there is a season,
and a time to every purpose under the heaven."*
(ECCLESIASTES 3:1)

STORY

Faith decided to do some journaling as a way of digging deeper into her purpose and discovering true contentment in her present state. Complaining did not lead to resolution. Making excuses became a crutch. Comparing herself to others was depressing. Her lack of productivity began to feel like a sin. She believed that committing to developing patience would give her a brand-new lease on life.

132

In her time of reflection and prayer, she learned about life's seasons. She learned how to enjoy the summer season that embodies youthful energy. Summer is the time to explore interests, gifts, and talents as well as bask in the sun while stimulating your thinking and invigorating your spirit. This can determine your level of enthusiasm and effectiveness, which can invite opportunities unimagined.

In the spring of your life, expect growth and welcome fresh ideas. Free your mind from all forces that work against your purpose for being created. This is not a time to conform, but a time to evolve and stand tall in your truth. Feed yourself wisdom from the Word that will equip you with the confidence to be uniquely you. Then you can show up strong and express yourself in your circle and your community.

Fall is the season to relish in the fruits of your labor. You are able to see and benefit from your hard work. You realize that taking time to plan and educate yourself on the unknown was not in vain. The criticisms and failures were all a part of the process. The pace becomes steady, and for the first time, you can see the light at the end of tunnel.

Finally, when winter comes, you have no regrets because you were 100% present in the seasons prior. Things have quieted down quite a bit and a shift has occurred. The atmosphere is cool and still by design. Strength is waning, and it is time for rest and rejuvenation. You are able to see things you could not see when life was loud and daylight was long. It is time to slow down, disconnect, and reflect. It is time to let some things fall by the wayside in order to absorb all that this season has for you. You are able to hear God without distraction because you recognize the sweetness of His voice because you sat with Him. Wear your hat of wisdom with pride; someone will appreciate your knowledge and insight in the days ahead.

When the purpose of life's seasons became clear to Faith, she felt much less stressful. She began to embrace each season as a time for reflection and rejuvenation.

APPLICATON

After spending quality time with God and reflecting on His goodness, you will know that He is the only one who can fill your void and sustain your joy! You will be able to proclaim with true conviction, "Thank you, God, for allowing me to embrace each season and see all that You have created me to be from Your perspective."

You are not promised a journey void of pain and suffering. However, your appreciation of life, or the lack thereof, is largely based on how you respond to it. It is helpful to consider what season you are in as you draw conclusions and make plans for your future. Discover your season and embrace the reality of it and all the intricacies that it brings. Patience is a virtue, and commitment brings forth fruit that creates spiritual health that will last a lifetime.

PRAYER

Lord, I thank You for helping me to surrender to You. Thank You for carrying me through the challenges that I must face. Most times, I am my biggest challenge. Help me not to compare myself to others or want what others have. Help me to understand that I am exactly where You would have me to be. Thank You for helping me appreciate my uniqueness and understand my value to You. Let me press into You so that my identity, affirmation, and purpose will come from You. Let me to not lean on the arm of the flesh but turn my heart completely to You. In Jesus' name, I praise You and thank You, Amen.

DAY 5

WRITE THE VISION

Do you know the power of the words in front of you?

"And the Lord answered me, and said, Write the vision, and make it plain on tables, that he may run that readeth it."
(HABAKKUK 2:2)

STORY

On New Year's Eve, Faith attended a vision board party and created a board outlining her goals. On the board, she glued the letters "PhD." To the right of that was the phrase, "Learn to change the world." Upon returning home, she placed the vision board in the corner and left it there for months. Three-fourths of the way into the year, her pastor preached a sermon on facing your fears. The sermon reminded her of the vision board, but she left it in the corner.

Faith's children were no longer babies, and she found herself navigating through a new season in life. She was fed up with her current employment status and feeling like there must be more to her vocational purpose. The sermon gave her renewed strength to return to school. The application process was arduous. She needed a comprehensive resume, transcripts from each college, essays, and letters of recommendations.

Finally, she dusted off that vision board and her goal for returning to school was right there. She had forgotten, but God had not. With unwavering faith, she dove into an academic process that would take an immeasurable amount of time and courage to complete. Regardless of all the obstacles that were in front of her, she was committed to facing her fear of becoming a student again.

APPLICATION

Do you have goals that you need to dust off? Are you tired of the status quo? Do you want to make a change in any area of your life but feel crippled and locked into bad decisions of the past? Write the vision and make it plain. Set a date to complete your goal. Otherwise, it is just a dream. Understand that God is the one who births a desire in you to soar, and He is more than capable of seeing His plan to fruition.

It is easy to remain true to the familiar. On the contrary, it takes a deep-seated belief in God and a strong commitment to live out your purpose and break free from habitual behavior.

Decide to rise up in the power of God and do the impossible. It is time to tread deeper waters and climb higher mountains in order for God to show Himself all-powerful in your life.

It is humbling and it can be intimidating, but God has a plan larger than what you could ever hope, dream, or imagine. Trust Him in your marriage, in your singleness, with your heavy heart, for your healing, as well as for strength to get through discouraging seasons and graciously evolve into a better person for His glory. Because of your decision to persevere against all odds, the final reward will far outweigh life's disappointments and struggles. Be the change that you want to see by committing to the process of writing the vision and walking out your prayers!

PRAYER

Oh Lord, I thank You for bringing the scriptures to life for me to hold onto firmly. Forgive me for opening the door to fear. I know that without faith, it is impossible to please You. Help me to lay fear at Your feet and leave it there. Thank You for allowing me to speak the Word over my life, expect change, and be committed to the work that brings results. You said that if we have faith the size of a mustard seed, we can speak to mountains and they will be moved. Thank You, Father for allowing me to lay my plans before You so that You may direct me each day. In Jesus' name, I pray, Amen.

JANUARY
WEEK 8

DAY 1
A GOOD DREAM

Whom am I helping?

"For all have sinned, and come short of the glory of God;
Being justified freely by his grace through
the redemption that is in Christ Jesus."
(ROMANS 3:23-24)

STORY

Michelle was exhausted and angry as she stood in the line, her cart overflowing with groceries. "Why am I feeling this way?" she thought.

Michelle had always been the "good girl." It was always her dream to be liked. She dreamed of being one of those people that generations

would look back on and marvel at her goodness. She was reliable, did what she was told, and always offered to help others no matter what.

"I am helping, but instead of joy, all I feel is resentment," she mumbled to herself.

APPLICATION

Humankind cannot receive salvation of their own accord. We all fall short. We are like horses at a racetrack chasing a bunny that will always be out of our reach. That rabbit's only purpose is to get the horses to run as fast as they can. The horses will always fall short because that is how it is designed to work.

The Bible emphasizes that our work will never be enough for salvation. This means that the work of salvation is God's. We must accept the gift. Imagine trying to give someone a gift because of your love, and instead of graciously accepting it, you are offered money for it. That defeats the purpose of giving a gift! Let us be grateful recipients of God's wonderful gift.

PRAYER

Father, help me to graciously accept the gift of grace that You have offered me. Help me not to strive in vain to gain something that I already have. I want to replace my dream of being seen as good by others with the dream of pleasing You with my heart. Lord, I want to serve and love others. I ask that you help me to give that service from a grateful heart. In Jesus' name, Amen.

DAY 2
DREAM OR NIGHTMARE

Why am I helping?

*"All the ways of a man are clean in his own eyes;
but the Lord weigheth the spirits."*
(PROVERBS 16:2)

STORY

Michelle's cousin had just graduated high school. Her aunt called and asked Michelle if she could help with the food for the celebration.

"Sure! Actually, Auntie, I'll just cover all of the food," Michelle enthusiastically offered. Michelle figured that taking any opportunity to be good and serve would help her accomplish this dream of being viewed by others as a "good person."

"Thank you so much, Michelle. You have such a servant's heart. You always have, even since you were a little girl," her aunt exclaimed.

Michelle felt the familiar flood of joy that came with such validating words. Now, standing in this line with at least $200 worth of groceries for the party that she really could not afford, that joy had worn off completely. All that was left was a feeling of bitterness.

APPLICATION

The Bible tells us that God knows what is in the heart of man. It may be easy to conceal your true feelings from others. You can put on a smile and act happy on the outside when there is, in fact, a storm raging on the inside. The only way most people know what another is thinking or feeling is if that person shares it honestly.

It is not this way with the Lord. No matter what face we put on, God knows what is brewing on the inside. This shows us that God knows the motives behind every action, every word spoken, and every good deed done. When you serve from a heart that wants to earn approval or earn the love of God or others, it is not authentic. While others may not know the contents of your heart, the Lord does.

PRAYER

Lord, help me to remember that You see my heart. When I am tempted to show something on the outside that is not true on the inside, help me to tell the truth in love to others. Help me to be honest with You, others, and myself about my motives and heart. Lord, help me to remember that I am loved and accepted by You. In Jesus' name, Amen.

DAY 3
WAKE ME UP

Do I know what I have?

*"For by grace are ye saved through faith;
and that not of yourselves: it is the gift of God."*
(EPHESIANS 2:8)

STORY

As far as Michelle could remember, she was always the "good girl." She was the one who obeyed her parents and teachers, and she was the model of behavior for all the other children to follow. Being a good girl was as much of Michelle's identity as being a Christian was. If she even thought someone was not pleased with her, she would develop an anxious pit in her stomach.

It was this way with God as well. Anytime Michelle fell short, lost her temper, gossiped, lied, or sinned in any way, she was overcome with guilt. She would repent repeatedly for the same sin. Michelle's dream of being good was starting to feel more like a nightmare. The only thing that seemed to resolve the feeling was to go out and do something nice for someone. Michelle had adopted this pattern.

"Where is this joy I should be feeling? Jesus, I know I am saved. Why do I feel bound?" Michelle thought.

She finally decided to open up to someone about her struggles. She called her good friend and the woman who had led her to Christ, Paula.

APPLICATION

The idea of a gift conjures the feelings of joy, excitement, surprise, and gratefulness. Most people like to get gifts. God has given us a gift. This gift is not like most. It will not break. It will not tear. It will not stop working. It will not need new batteries. The warranty will never run out.

God gave the gift of salvation. This gift also comes with freedom. It is a freedom not to have to work and strive for God's love and acceptance. The work is already done. Jesus did a hard, bloody, painful, and lonely work for us on the cross. His work has allowed us to receive the gift that keeps on giving!

PRAYER

Lord, thank You for the gift that keeps on giving. This is a wonderful blessing, and I want to honor You with it. Help me accept the freedom that comes with such a gift, the freedom not to strive for Your love. Help me to relish and rest in that freedom and cherish your wonderful gift. In Jesus' name, Amen.

DAY 4

RELEASING THE DREAM

How do I accept God's good gift?

"As every man hath received the gift,
even so minister the same one to another,
as good stewards of the manifold grace of God."
(I PETER 4:10)

STORY

As soon as Paula answered, the words poured out of Michelle's mouth like a faucet. "I'm miserable! I work so much for others. I do as much as I can to serve and please the Lord, but all I feel is emptiness. It's like I'm climbing a mountain with a ten-ton weight on my back! I have always had this dream of being seen as

'good' by others, but right now I think I just need someone to wake me up."

"Wow, Michelle," Paula said. "You have been carrying a heavy burden. You know I love you, but it sounds like you are doing things to try to earn some sort of righteousness. Girl, God's forgiving grace is a gift. If you do something for someone, let it be because you are so grateful for God's gift that you give and serve out of a loving heart and not one that desires validation. You cannot do enough to earn forgiveness. Jesus shed His blood for this. He already carried that burden. Go ahead and wake up, girl!"

APPLICATION

Many have heard of the concept of "paying it forward." The premise is that doing something nice for people inspires them to do something nice for others. God is the originator of "paying it forward." He gives us the wonderful gift of salvation through grace. When God's gift is accepted, we should be inspired to bless others from a heart overflowing with gratefulness. When we accept God's gift, it frees us to love and serve others authentically.

PRAYER

Father, thank You so much for the wonderful gift of salvation that You have given me. I ask that You help me to live out my gratefulness in loving service to others. Help me to pay it forward in a way that honors You! In Jesus' name, Amen.

DAY 5
A NEW DREAM

How do I live differently in light of God's gift?

"Let us therefore come boldly unto the throne of grace,
that we may obtain mercy,
and find grace to help in time of need."
(HEBREWS 4:16)

STORY

Michelle was stunned. No one had ever called her out on serving for the purpose of receiving validation. People mostly seemed more than eager to accept Michelle's help and throw plenty of compliments her way.

"Thank you, Paula. That really hit home. I need to go somewhere and pray now!" Michelle cried.

"Anytime, friend! You know I'm here for you," Paula said.

Michelle knew the moment she hung up the phone that it was time to walk in God's gift and let her service flow from a grateful heart, not to earn or prove anything to anyone. Finally, Michelle felt grateful. She was awake now; she knew that it was time to pursue a new dream. This time, the dream would be to have a heart that was motivated to please God and Him alone. Waking up felt great!

APPLICATION

The words "bold" and "grace" may seem strange when placed together in the same sentence. The Bible tells us that because of God's grace towards us, we can come to Him boldly.

When someone goes to their house and pulls out the key to open the door, they do not do so hesitantly. Most are confident that their key will work to get into their house. This is the place where they live. Therefore, they enter it boldly because they know they have a right to be there. In the same way, God has given us a key to His throne of grace. He wants us to use that key to come boldly to Him for an unending flow of grace and mercy. Accepting God's gift enables us to come boldly before the throne!

PRAYER

Lord, thank You for entrusting me with the key to come before your throne. Help me to enter into Your presence, knowing that I am loved and accepted and that I can never exhaust Your grace and mercy. In Jesus' name, Amen.

JANUARY
WEEK 9

DAY 1

RISING ABOVE DISAPPOINTMENTS

Can you believe that happened?

*"And we know that all things work together
for good to them that love God,
to them who are the called according to his purpose."*
(ROMANS 8:28)

STORY

Monique and Charles had been married for ten years. The marriage was not perfect, but Monique thought they were happy. To Monique's shock and dismay, Charles came home one day and told her that he no longer wanted to be married. Monique was crushed. She questioned herself. She questioned God. She felt as though her life was over.

Monique's relationship with the Lord had been casual at best. She attended church at least twice a month, but she had slacked off on her personal devotion and prayer time. This situation with Charles caused Monique to deepen her relationship with the Lord. She also reached out to a Christian counselor to get support and advice.

APPLICATION

Sometimes, we experience various hardships in life. Life comes at us quickly. Nevertheless, when we least expect it, things can end up working together for our good. Recall a time when you experienced a major disappointment, life challenge or adversity. How did God end up using your disappointment to cause everything to work together for good in your life?

PRAYER

Dear Lord, it never feels good when going through hard times. Even though we do not always understand why things happen, I am glad that I can trust You through the hard times. Help me to see Your hand in the midst of everything that I go through. Although the situation may not be good, I know that You will work it out for my good. In Jesus' name, I pray, Amen.

DAY 2

RISING ABOVE SICKNESS

Can you believe that there is healing for you?

"Beloved, I wish above all things that thou mayest prosper and be in health, even as thy soul prospereth."
(III JOHN 1:2)

STORY

The phone rang. Monique's mom was on the other end. Monique's heart sank when she heard her mom share that her dad had taken another fall. Since his previous illness, it had been difficult for her dad to maintain his balance. This time, the fall caused a disc in his hip to slip.

Her dad was in the hospital, and Monique rushed to be by his side. When she arrived, he was in good spirits as always. He always had a strong faith in God. Even though he was in pain, he encouraged Monique and told her to trust in the Lord.

A P P L I C A T I O N

Are you one to see the proverbial glass half-empty or half full? Our soul prospers when we have lives that are committed to spiritual development. It is important to train our souls to prosper in the things of God by walking in the fruit of the Spirit, spending time in prayer, and seeking guidance and direction from the Bible. When this happens, it gives us a prosperous outlook for our mind, body, and spirit.

Take some time to engage in soul-searching and look for ways to have a prosperous soul. How does your prosperous soul affect your mind and your body? Make a prosperity list.

P R A Y E R

Dear Lord, I desire to be prosperous in every aspect of my life. Teach me to train my mind, my body, and my soul to walk in divine prosperity so that I am able to bloom, to thrive, and to advance forward into everything that You have purposed for my life. I give You praise and glory. In Jesus' name, I pray, Amen.

DAY 3
RISING ABOVE DELAYS

Can you wait on Him?

*"But, beloved, be not ignorant of this one thing,
that one day is with the Lord as a thousand years,
and a thousand years as one day."*
(II PETER 3:8)

STORY

Monique had been at her job for five years. She felt that it was time to move up to another position. She saw a position posted in the human resource department that interested her. She had applied for new positions in the past, but nothing had come of it. She was tired of waiting. She decided that she would apply for this position, and if she did not get it, she was willing to clean out her desk and seek a job in a different company.

Monique applied for the open position. Unfortunately, one of her co-workers filled the position. She was heart-broken and had to make a decision about her next move.

APPLICATION

Waiting on God is one of the most difficult things that we have to do. Like children, we want what we want when we want it. Therefore, we might pout. We might whine. We might determine to make things happen on our own. Our childish tactics do not move God. He has a reason for everything and always knows what is best for us.

Have you ever tried to rush God? What were the consequences? What are you waiting on right now? Ask God how He wants to grow you while you wait. Determine that there is purpose in the *meantime season* of your life so that you can wait patiently on Him.

PRAYER

Lord, waiting is so hard. It is hard because I believe I know what is best for me at any given time. Forgive me, Lord. Help me to trust You and to know there is a purpose behind my waiting. Thank You for Your promise that says that no one who trusts in You will be put to shame. In Jesus' name, I pray, Amen.

DAY 4

RISING ABOVE COMPARISONS

Can you believe that you are good enough?

*"I will praise thee;
for I am fearfully and wonderfully made:
marvellous are thy works;
and that my soul knoweth right well."*
(PSALM 139:14)

STORY

Monique, Sherry, and Dasia had been friends since elementary school. When people saw one, they usually saw the others. They were like three peas in a pod. Monique always felt Sherry was the prettiest and Dasia was the smartest. She saw herself as the outcast of the group. Her arms and legs were long and lanky. Her hair was thick and hard to manage. Her grades were average at best.

Sherry had a wonderful husband and two cute kids. Dasia was a leader in her department on her job and always excelled in her career. Even though Sherry and Dasia saw all three of them as equals, Monique struggled with seeing herself in a positive light, especially with the recent break up from her husband Mark. Sherry and Dasia often encouraged Monique, telling her that they loved her just for who she was.

APPLICATION

As women, many times it is difficult to see our own value. We see "her" as thinner, taller, smarter, funnier, more spiritual, and on and on. God does all things well, including His artisanship of you and me. In fact, we insult God when we do not value His work of art. Find scriptures that speak to your value and worth. Insert your name into each verse, and then remind yourself daily that you are fearfully and wonderfully made in His image.

PRAYER

Lord, You do all things well. I am sorry that I have not always seen myself as worthy or good enough. I desire to please You at all times, and pleasing You means seeking to imitate You and You only. I commit to counting my blessings and not the blessings of others. You are no respecter of persons, and You love me just as much. Thank You for fearfully and wonderfully making me. Wonderful are Your works. In Jesus' name, I pray, Amen.

DAY 5
RISING ABOVE FEARS

Can you stand and not be afraid?

*"For God hath not given us the spirit of fear;
but of power, and of love,
and of a sound mind."*
(II TIMOTHY 1:7)

STORY

Monique liked to have coffee with her neighbor Janice on the weekends. Janice had been serving as the neighborhood association president for the past two years. Her term was ending. Janice suggested that Monique should take over as the new president.

Monique almost choked on her coffee when Janice suggested it. The last thing that Monique was comfortable doing was serving in a leadership role and having to speak in front of her neighbors. Janice assured Monique that she was well-qualified for the role. She knew the issues. She had lived in the neighborhood for many years, and all of the neighbors loved her. Monique, on the other hand, felt a great amount of fear just thinking about the possibility of serving in this role.

APPLICATION

Have you ever experienced paralyzing fear? It is the kind of fear that causes your palms to sweat, your heart to beat fast, and your mind to race. Guess what? Fear and faith cannot reside in the same space. It is normal to feel apprehension and uneasiness.

Faith in God will push fear out of the way. Fear does not come from God. He gives us supernatural power to overcome situations, supernatural love to operate in the midst of every situation, and self-discipline to guide us through our situations.

What causes your fear? Replace every fear with faith. Create a faith journal to record all of the magnificent things that the Lord has seen you through in life.

PRAYER

Lord, sometimes fear overtakes me. Teach me to walk in faith. You told Joshua not to be afraid and not to be discouraged. You promised to be with him wherever he went. I am standing on the power of Your Word. You promised that Your Word would not return empty without accomplishing great things. I am fearless in You. I am bold in You. I am faith-filled in You. In Jesus' name, I pray, Amen.

FEBRUARY
WEEK 10

DAY 1

HOUSE OF COMFORT

What is the cost of kindness?

"And the barbarous people shewed us no little kindness: for they kindled a fire, and received us everyone, because of the present rain, and because of the cold."
(ACTS 28:2)

STORY

It was an early November morning. Jazmin had just returned home from dropping her two kids off at school. She was getting a cup of coffee when her husband Stan came into the kitchen with a stunned look on his face. After Jazmin asked him what was going on, he proceeded to tell her the story of a young family in their church who had just been in a

house fire. Jazmin's heart sank as she thought of how traumatic it must be for the couple's two children to have experienced the fire and now to be out of their home for a while.

Stan's next words left Jazmin feeling completely distressed. "They can come stay with us. You know they don't have family here, and the kids would love the company," he suggested in an enthusiastic tone.

Jazmin's emotions went from panic to guilt as thoughts raced through her mind. "I'd love to help Lord, but am I ready for a house full of guests? Do we even have room for all of them? We don't even know them that well. What kind of Christian am I for thinking like this?"

APPLICATION

At times in our Christian walk, we may find ourselves asking the Lord to use us so that we can experience His power in some way. Yet, when the invitation comes to do something good on behalf of others, which demonstrates the power of His love, we may find that this will cost us more than we are willing to pay.

To be used of the Lord is rarely comfortable or easy. This is especially true when you are given an opportunity to show hospitality to other believers or those in need. When you open your house up to others, you are being vulnerable, allowing them to observe you through a different lens. A woman's home is like her sanctuary, the refuge and safe space for her family. Opening your house to others is a sign of humility, love and trust in the Lord.

Inviting others into your home may expose you to their opinions, but it is also an intimate way to touch their hearts with God's loving-kindness. Scripture tells us that when we do good and share with others what we have, these sacrifices please Him.

When you accept an opportunity to show hospitality, you can trust that the Lord's reward will far outweigh anything you feel you have given up. As you open your house to bless others, God is fulfilling your heart's desire to be used by Him.

PRAYER

Father God, when I am given an opportunity to open my house to others, please teach me to love them the way You do. When I am overly stressed and feel vulnerable over what my guests may think of my home, help me to focus on serving them as if I am serving You. Give me Your peace as I prepare my home to welcome those who need Your refreshing and encouragement. Give me creative ideas that will set an atmosphere in my home that brings joy, peace, and comfort to those who come through the doors. Show me practical ways to express Your love and kindness in my conversation and my actions. Remind me that as I show hospitality to other believers or those in need, You are watching and are pleased with me. In the name of Jesus, Amen.

DAY 2

DOORS OF OPPORTUNITY

Do you want to show off or show up?

"But Martha was cumbered about much serving, and came to him, and said, Lord, dost thou not care that my sister hath left me to serve alone? Bid her therefore that she help me."
(LUKE 10:40)

STORY

Jazmin began putting the new Egyptian cotton sheets on the bed that would be offered to the couple coming to stay. Making mental notes of all that needed to be done to prepare for the family of four arriving by noon, she was beginning to feel anxious.

Just then, Stan walked in. "Here you are," he smiled. Glancing over at the queen-sized sleigh bed, he asked, "Wow, are these new sheets? They feel so nice." He rubbed the fabric between his fingers. "Shoot, we need these on our bed!" he exclaimed with a sly grin. "Babe, the Jacksons will be happy with having a place to stay; they won't even care about this fancy stuff."

Hunching her shoulders while stating her case, Jazmin responded, "I know, but how often do we have people from the church come to our house, let alone stay the night. We don't even know how long they will be here. I just want to make sure everything is right. This house represents me."

"I hear you," Stan responded as he left the room.

As Jazmin floated through the house, preparing every room, she whispered to herself, "Lord, I want to do what's right, but this feels overwhelming."

APPLICATION

When we are expecting guests in our home, we can easily get distracted in making sure the house is together and become frazzled in the process. Many of us find ourselves scurrying around the house tidying up before anyone steps foot across the doorway!

After all, our home is a representation of our private lives, revealing our style, our personality, and even our cleaning habits! As Christians, we should be attentive to taking care of our houses, as we see in scripture where the older women are encouraged to teach the younger women to be keepers of their homes.

It is hard to show true authentic care and concern for your guests when you are panicked about having the right dishes, the best guest towels, or other home decor elements. If you think your house is not good enough to invite others, you will pass on the opportunity to be hospitable.

The Lord knows the motives of our hearts. He knows whether we are showing off to impress people or showing up to serve others. If our focus is on the place, rather than the people, we miss the blessing.

While getting the house ready, take a moment and focus on how you want your guests to feel after they leave. Pray as you walk through your home, asking the Lord to give you ideas to make your guests' experience special. When you ask God for help, He will give you peace and the grace to enjoy your company.

PRAYER

Father God, give me a heart to serve those who enter my home. Help me to focus on meeting their needs rather than on getting my house prepared. When I start to get anxious, remind me that I am a conduit of Your love towards the guests in my home. I desire to be a blessing to all who pass through my doors. May they sense Your peace within these walls. Give me ideas to create an atmosphere that is welcoming and loving. When I get weary while showing hospitality, remind me that as I serve my guests, I am serving You. Lord, search my heart. If there are any selfish, prideful, and wrong motives in me, change me. May I represent You as I host those who are special to You. In the name of Jesus, Amen.

DAY 3

WALLS OF RESISTANCE

Are you ready for change?

*"And whatsoever ye do, do it heartily,
as to the Lord, and not unto men;
Knowing that of the Lord ye shall receive the reward
of the inheritance: for ye serve the Lord Christ."*
(COLOSSIANS 3:23-24)

STORY

Whew, what a day! The Jacksons seem so happy to be here," Jazmin stated with relief, taking off her shoes, while Stan turned on the shower.

"I know. I told you this would be a good thing," Stan replied.

"And the kids are enjoying this new living arrangement," Jazmin interrupted. "Shannon was just telling me that her kids were so excited to come because they know Bella and Justin from children's church."

Just then, the phone rang. "Hey, Mom!" Jazmin answered excitedly. "Things are great. We have a family from church staying with us," she said as a matter-of-fact. Taking the phone into the walk-in closet, she continued, "Well, no we don't know them that well, but…" Her countenance changed as she talked. "Stan knows the husband from church and his wife Shannon seems really friendly." Jazmin stopped in her tracks, "Well, Mom I have a peace about it," she continued in a defensive voice. "Look, Mom, I've got to go," Jazmin said and hung up abruptly. Turning to Stan, she said in a defeated tone, "Mom's concerned that we have strangers in our home."

"Honey, we have to learn to hear the Lord for ourselves," he reminded her.

APPLICATION

Whenever we choose to obey the Lord, there will often be opposition and resistance either from doubt in our own hearts or from others. It is at these times when we must do a heart check to examine our motives. Are we seeking to please the Lord or to satisfy other people's opinions?

Practicing hospitality is a very personal way to serve the Lord. This is especially true when you invite strangers or those who are not in your immediate circle to visit or stay in your home. Even though we have to use wisdom in deciding whom we allow around our family, it is important to be led by the Lord, who will give you peace about your decision.

The Word of God reminds us that those who are led by the Spirit of God are the sons of God. In our Christian journey, we may experience the Lord's nudging to do something others may not understand. The Lord sees when we go against other's opinions to act on His instructions.

Choosing to be hospitable will require a change in mindset. It is not for others to validate your decision to obey, but for you to trust that the Lord has led you.

PRAYER

Father God, help me to hear Your voice as You invite me to extend my heart and home to others in need. Change any wrong mindset that might hinder me from obeying You. Give me wisdom to know whom to allow around my family. Teach me to trust Your leading in opening my home to those I may not know. When resistance comes from others' opinions or my own doubts, help me to stand firm in my obedience to You. As I obey Your nudging to be hospitable, train me to sense Your peace so that I can move forward to serve my guests as unto You. Search my heart so that I may be led by Your Spirit and not swayed by the opinions of others. Help me to take courage in knowing that You are working through me to bless others. In the name of Jesus, Amen.

DAY 4
WINDOWS OF BLESSINGS

Are you ready to receive?

"Be not forgetful to entertain strangers:
for thereby some have entertained angels unawares."
(HEBREWS 13:2)

STORY

"What's that noise?" Jazmin exclaimed, waking from her sleep.

"It is 7:00 a.m.," Stan reported, getting up to investigate.

"Sounds like the vacuum cleaner," Jazmin said as she got into her robe.

They followed the sound that led right to the Jackson kids' room. There behind the vacuum cleaner was the elder of the Jackson kids, a daughter only ten years old pushing the machine like an experienced pro. "Good morning!" Jazmin yelled over the humming of the vacuum.

"Mornin'!" shouted the little guy in the bathroom wiping down the counters.

"You kids are amazing!" Stan confirmed with a big grin.

Just then, the parents of the two cleaning bandits popped into the room, smiling as their eyes met their children.

"Son, don't forget to empty the trash," the dad reminded the eight-year-old, who began pulling up the liner from the wastebasket.

"Wow, I'm amazed! One week here and you guys are blessing us," Jazmin proclaimed.

"We do this every Saturday; it's our job. Mom says that our chores don't stop because we're here," the little guy commented.

"Maybe you can spread this cleaning bug to your sleeping friends!" Stan encouraged, as they all laughed.

APPLICATION

Opening your home to others is a practical way to show unconditional love, especially when it is to people you do not really know or who may not be able to reciprocate that blessing. The Word challenges us not to only invite those in our homes who are in our friend groups or families, but also to extend hospitality to those who are outside our familiar circles.

The gift of hospitality includes entertaining, eating, enjoying conversation, and inviting others to stay during a difficult season. The inconvenience of the cleaning, serving, and cooking is easily leveraged with the joy of the fellowship of your guests. Is it not just like our heavenly Father to suggest in His Word that this should be the practice of those desiring to be leaders in the church?

You can trust that any inconvenience experienced in serving others for the Lord's sake will be exchanged for a blessing. When you open yourself to be used by God, He may even give you your heart's desire in a way you least expect it. The Lord may even use the guests in your home to bring about the answer to the requests you have made of Him. It is like a divine exchange. The windows of blessings are opened to us as we open our hearts to show His compassion.

PRAYER

Father God, open my eyes that I may see the principles You are teaching me by practicing hospitality. Give me Your heart for those who are not in my social circles who need Your compassion. May the guests in my home experience Your love, as they are welcomed with warmth, kindness, and fellowship. Help me to grow in my love walk as I seek to open myself and my home to others. Show me creative and practical ways to go above and beyond the expectations of my guests so they will leave having experienced authentic and gracious fellowship. Teach me how to be open to Your invitations to join You in loving on those who need to know and experience You personally. Remind me that You are the ultimate giver, and I am Your servant, offering what I have to be a blessing. In the name of Jesus, Amen.

DAY 5
ROOF OF LOVE
Who is covered?

"And above all things have fervent charity among yourselves: for charity shall cover the multitude of sins. Use hospitality one to another without grudging. As every man hath received the gift, even to minister the same one to another, as good stewards of the manifold grace of God."
(I PETER 4:8-10)

STORY

So, you're all packed up?" Jazmin asked, plopping down on the couch.

"Yep, all packed!" Shannon answered while folding the last load of clothes. "You know Jazmin, I don't know what God has in store for

you and Stan, but I know it's going to be great," she said becoming emotional. "After the fire happened, we knew the insurance would cover living expenses, but I told my husband, I can't imagine our kids staying in a hotel for over two weeks. You and Stan pretty much laid out the red carpet for us. We can't thank you enough for your open arms towards us," Shannon shared through the tears.

Jazmin responded, "Girl, it's been a life-changing experience for me! Before you all got here, I was in a desert place with the Lord, feeling lonely and unfulfilled. I had just told God, the week before you came, that I needed to see Him do something in my life. Your family being here has been an answered prayer. Your kids have made chores a fun adventure for our kids, not to mention, the Lord gave me and Stan good friends in the process!"

APPLICATION

What an amazing opportunity it is to use our homes to minister to people. As believers, we all need people we can count on to open their homes for casual fellowship or to provide a place to stay in hard times.

Through hospitality, we get to observe the Body of Christ functioning in the love of God in a real and practical way. Scripture points out that if one member of the body suffers, all the members suffer with it. As Christians we are interdependent; simply put, we need each other. The Word tells us that two people are better than one because when one falls, there is someone to pick him up.

Hospitality allows you to support, build up and serve fellow believers and others. The unselfish act of your hospitality often means sacrificing your time, resources, and privacy. Under your roof, the love of the Lord is on display. It affects you and your guests, long after the visit is over. You both get to experience aspects of God's character.

As you host others, the Lord's compassion is shown as you create an atmosphere that encourages unity in relationships. Your guests get to experience God's grace through the warm, comforting environment of your home with no strings attached. In this way, both parties thrive as they experience the giving and receiving of God's unconditional love.

PRAYER

Father God, thank You for the honor and privilege to minister to the needs of others using the atmosphere of my home. When practicing hospitality becomes uncomfortable or an inconvenience, remind me that I have an opportunity to be used to entertain, serve, and refresh those who come to visit or stay in my home. Allow me to see the bigger picture in sacrificing my personal space, resources, and time to bless my guests. Lord, help me to make hospitality a part of my lifestyle consistently. Give me a humble heart to remember that we all need others for support and encouragement in times of need. As a part of the Body of Christ, may I always be available to open my heart and home to those You want to experience Your unconditional love. In the name of Jesus, Amen.

FEBRUARY
WEEK 11

DAY 1
HEAL MY HEART

Will my brokenness be restored?

*"The LORD is nigh unto them that are of a broken heart;
and saveth such as be of a contrite spirit."*
(PSALMS 34:18)

STORY

Cheryl and Sandra met at a restaurant for their monthly girlfriends' lunch date. They used this time together to catch up on what was going on in their lives and to encourage each other. This time their standing luncheon date fell on Valentine's Day. Sandra was glad that Cheryl did not cancel.

"Cheryl, thank you for taking some time away from your husband to meet with me. I hope I am not interfering with your plans for this special day," Sandra said.

"No problem. Sam and I aren't celebrating Valentine's Day until later this evening," Cheryl responded. "I am surprised we were able to get a reservation at all because restaurants are always packed."

Every year, Cheryl's husband Sam made a big deal of celebrating Valentine's Day by treating his wife to a fancy dinner and buying her lavish gifts. Although Cheryl always felt that he went overboard, she eagerly looked forward to his surprises. Sam always did something special that touched her heart.

"You two are so cute," Sandra smiled. "I was hoping this meeting would also be a celebration. I can't believe I didn't get this job either! I feel stuck professionally."

Sandra had the education and work experience that matched the job description and requirements perfectly. She had done everything the career experts suggested, including going back to school to earn an additional degree. Before applying, she prayed about every position and her interviews all went well. Though she was excited about each new position, she was constantly disappointed when she was not selected. She had been in her current position for ten years and could not seem to move forward.

"Why do I keep punishing myself?" she asked Cheryl. "I am thankful for my current job, but I thought God had something more for me. I guess I was wrong. Being in this situation breaks my heart."

Reaching across the table to hold her friend's hands, Cheryl said, "Sandra, God wants to heal our brokenness, and that includes our heartbreaks and disappointments in life."

Cheryl shared with Sandra that she and Sam would not be celebrating Valentine's Day had they not experienced a few heartbreaks and disappointments along the way. She promised Sandra that she would get through this, reminding her that God remains close to the brokenhearted.

"Thank you for being a listening ear and reminding me of God's goodness and His promises," Sandra said. "Please pray that I am able to discern what God has in store for my professional future and that He heals my broken heart.

"Of course, I will always be a listening ear for you, and I will continue to pray for you. Give the Lord the pieces of your heart and wait for Him to restore it. We will celebrate that new job before you know it!" Cheryl said enthusiastically.

Sandra remembered it was Valentine's Day. She told herself that each time she saw a heart she would let it serve as a reminder of God's love for her.

APPLICATION

All of us have been disappointed. All of us have been confident in an expected outcome only to have our hopes dashed. It is okay to feel sadness when things do not work out as planned. God warned us that heartaches were going to happen. We must be careful to avoid falling into the trap of self-pity during those times.

The Bible says that He saves those with a contrite spirit. A contrite spirit is one that is crushed and broken. To move past the brokenness requires getting into a position to be saved. He does not discard us in our despair. God promises that He is close to us at all times. Always remember that the Lord is near to us in our disappointments; He will indeed save us.

PRAYER

Dear Lord, help me to remember that You see me in my brokenness. You are with me in the good times and the bad times. Thank You for never leaving my side. My brokenness is temporary. Your love for me is eternal. I give You my heart and the circumstances that have caused it to break. I know You will restore me. You will heal me, and You will save me. Thank You for loving me. In Jesus' name, I pray, Amen.

DAY 2
SEARCH MY HEART

Do my desires please the Lord?

"Search me, O God, and know my heart!
Try me and know my thoughts!"
(PSALMS 139:23)

Sandra called Cheryl to see how her Valentine's Day dinner went with Sam. After she heard all the juicy details, she asked Cheryl if she had a few moments to talk. She was thankful her friend took the time to listen.

"Cheryl, I have done some soul searching about my job hunt and my life in general. So many of my desires have been for my glory, my promotion, or my own recognition. Last night, I asked myself if my wants and desires honor the Lord. I realized that when I applied for all of those jobs, I was thinking about myself, not God."

Before Sandra applied for jobs, she looked at how they would benefit her financially and what perks would be available to her. Although her education and experience made her more than qualified, her heart was not qualified. She had forgotten that the Lord promotes for His glory, not ours. Sandra never took the time to think about how she could glorify God in the new jobs she wanted so desperately.

"Sandra, I like what I'm hearing." Cheryl beamed. "Your revelation doesn't just apply to job hunting. It applies to all aspects of our lives, including relationships."

Cheryl shared her testimony about how being selfish can keep you from God's will. She explained that she had a few bad relationships before she met Sam. She was always dating the jock, the looker, the dresser, and the popular men because they made her look good and people were impressed. Once God revealed her true motives, she put her selfish desires on the shelf. It was then that God blessed her with Sam, who exceeded her expectations.

Sandra thanked Cheryl for sharing her testimony. It encouraged her to look at every aspect of her life to determine if her thoughts and actions were honoring God or man. She now realized that when you surrender your heart's desires to the Lord, He will send you what you need.

APPLICATION

How much of what we do is for our glory? How many times have we picked up something and thought, "I can't wait for my friends to see me with this?" When we are asked to do something extra, do we ever think, "What is in this for me?" Why do we have those thoughts? Is it because we want to impress our friends and want others to admire our accomplishments and us?

Many of us make decisions based on what we will receive. We are often disappointed when we do not receive the desired reaction from our peers.

The "What's in it for me?" attitude is definitely not God's perspective. When we approach opportunities with ourselves in mind, we are stealing the glory from God. Take a moment and examine your actions. How much heartache would you avoid if you searched your heart before making a decision?

PRAYER

Dear Lord, You know my thoughts and my heart. You are acquainted with all my ways. Please align my head and my heart with Your Word and Your will. Help me to surrender my dreams and desires to You. I do not want anything that is not Your will for me. My desire is to live a life for Your glory. In Jesus' name, I pray, Amen.

DAY 3
KEEP MY HEART

Will my choices lead me to peace?

"Let not your hearts be troubled. Believe in God: believe also in me."
(JOHN 14:1)

STORY

Sandra saw another job that was of interest to her. She wondered if she should apply. The job description looked like it was written with her in mind. She thought about applying for it, but she had been down that road many times. Sandra picked up the phone and called Cheryl.

"Girl, I see a new job, and I want to apply for it," Sandra said calmly. "I have prayed about it, and I

feel like I have the right attitude and approach this time. I will not be anxious or troubled. If this job is for me, then it is for me."

"I cannot see into the future, but I know you will not go wrong believing in God's guidance," Cheryl responded excitedly.

Cheryl encouraged Sandra to follow the peace of God and apply for the job. She then explained to Sandra the peace she felt when she first met Sam. They were both tired of doing things their own ways and trusting God to lead them to a like-minded person, and He did.

"Is that why you always say that your relationship was free of the stressful situations most couples experience?" Sandra asked.

"Yes," Cheryl explained. "We had peace the entire time we were dating. Peace is a gift from God to calm your troubled heart. Continue to pray for guidance. I will support you and whatever you decide to do."

APPLICATION

You Only Live Once (YOLO) is a phrase people use when they sometimes make a spur of the moment decision. These choices are fun, but choices made in haste do not always bring you peace. On the flip side, we have all experienced the feeling of peace when we make a thoughtful decision. The peace that comes when we take time to listen to God is so much better than the angst that comes from making a decision in a hurry.

Believing God gives us the ability to make choices that bring us peace. We can rest when our actions reflect God's desires for us. Peace comes from God. God wants us to have His peace. Peace does not mean the outcome will always be what you are expecting, but it does mean that you believe the outcome is God's will for your life. Your heart will not be troubled when you trust and believe that God is in control.

P R A Y E R

Dear Lord, I know it is not Your desire for us to live a life full of regrets. We have all made poor decisions. Our lives are not meant to be lived in a reckless manner. Following You and Your Word leads us to peace. Believing in You stills my troubled heart. Thank You for Your love and Your guidance. In Jesus' name, I pray, Amen.

MY WHOLE HEART

Is my focus divided?

"With my whole heart I seek you;
let me not wander from your commandments."
(PSALMS 119:10)

STORY

Sandra felt that it was not in God's will for her to apply for the new position that she had discussed with Cheryl. She was not disappointed because she had decided to live her life to glorify God, not herself. A week after she came to this decision, she was informed that her company was opening a new department. Her supervisor asked her to lead the new department. The position came with a pay increase and did not require relocation. It was the perfect job for her.

After accepting the new role, Sandra called Cheryl to share the good news. "The job description matches my experience and skills perfectly. I will also continue to work with people I know and do some of the things I was hoping to do when I applied for those other jobs," she announced happily.

"Sandra, that is good news!" Cheryl screamed. "Congratulations! I am so happy for you. Did you know there was a possibility of promotion at your company?" Before Sandra could answer, she continued, "This makes so much sense. If you had been offered any of the jobs you applied for earlier, you would have missed this opportunity. You had to get your heart right before you could receive this amazing blessing. When do you start? More importantly, when do we get to celebrate?"

APPLICATION

Multitasking is considered by many to be an efficient way to manage time, but is it really? When we multitask, our focus is divided. How many times have we had to re-read a passage in a book because we were distracted by the television in the background? How many accidents has a distracted driver wandering off the road has caused? No one likes being with a person who is constantly doing something else. Giving a person your full attention shows them that you value them and their time.

If people and tasks deserve our full attention, then so does God. We cannot have a meaningful relationship with God if He does not have our whole heart. Once you release your expectations and surrender to God, He will open doors for you. When you seek His direction, He really does keep you from wandering off the path that He has set for you.

PRAYER

Dear Lord, You deserve my full attention. Please forgive me when I come to You distracted. I am sorry for the times I have wandered off the path You set before me. Help me to seek You with my whole heart. When my focus is on You, I stay on track. I promise to give You my whole heart and my undivided attention. In Jesus' name, I pray, Amen.

DAY 5
KNOW MY HEART

Will my plans lead me in the right direction?

*"Every way of a man is right in his own eyes:
but the Lord pondereth the hearts."*
(PROVERBS 21:2)

STORY

Cheryl and Sandra met up for their monthly girlfriends' lunch date. So much had happened since their last meeting. This time, Sandra had really gotten the job she wanted, and they had a reason to celebrate.

"Sandra, not only are we celebrating a new position for you, but, more importantly, we are

celebrating how God saved you during your time of brokenness," Cheryl said as she handed Sandra balloons and a congratulatory gift. Cheryl hugged her friend before taking her seat.

"Cheryl, I thought I knew how I should advance professionally," Sandra admitted. "My way was to look for a new place to work. I never even considered looking within my company for a new position. God knew better, of course. God knew in my heart that I was really looking for a promotion, not necessarily a new employer."

Over lunch, the two friends laughed about all the fun and not so fun moments they had shared. They were grateful to have each other for support and encouragement. They vowed never to end their lunch dates because they had such a positive impact on their lives and their friendship.

APPLICATION

We are creatures of habit. It is easy for us to be stuck in a rut, especially when things are going well. We believe that our way must be the right way. Many of us are hesitant to try new foods, visit new places, change our route to a frequently visited location, or even change our hairstyle. The list is endless.

How many of us have been pleasantly surprised after trying something new? We miss many opportunities by trying to be in control and by staying in our comfort zones. We do not have all of the answers within ourselves. God is the only one with all the answers. Only He knows our hearts. Only He knows all the details of our situations. We need to be open to the will of God, even when our way has been successful.

PRAYER

Dear Lord, thank You for giving me Your Word to lead and to guide me. You know my heart. My well-intentioned thoughts are fallible. My way may not be the best way or the right way. You are infallible. Lead me in the right direction as I surrender my will to You. Help me to follow your lead. In Jesus' name, I pray, Amen.

FEBRUARY
WEEK 12

DAY 1

MY BODY, MY TEMPLE, MY SPACE

How can I find the time to focus on me?

*"What? know ye not that your body
is the temple of the Holy Ghost which is in you,
which ye have of God, and ye are not your own?
For ye are bought with a price; therefore,
glorify God in your body, and in your spirit,
which are God's."*
(I CORINTHIANS 6:19-20)

STORY

Each morning Lisa would meet her friend Crystal for a walk, and sometimes they would jog. Some mornings they would walk for thirty minutes, but oftentimes they would walk for over an hour, hashing out the world's problems. They would share their worries, their fears, their dreams, their goals, and their concerns for their families and loved ones.

One morning, Lisa and Crystal engaged in deep prayer during their morning time together because Crystal's husband was undergoing a serious surgery later that day. They stopped in the middle of their walk to pray, mediate, and ask God for His divine covering of protection over Crystal's husband. After their prayer, Crystal expressed her frustration that her husband needed the surgery. If he had taken advantage of some preventive measures that had been recommended to him for several years, surgery could have been avoided.

Lisa and Crystal then began to encourage each other to continue their walks each morning, realizing that their long walks could prevent a health crisis from occurring within their own bodies. They expressed how much they enjoyed the quiet time in the mornings because it opened up a window for "girlfriend" time. They also realized and admitted that the morning walks were a necessary habit because they allowed time for God to speak to their spirits. Indeed, the walks were helping them to take care of their bodies, minds, and spirits.

APPLICATION

Girlfriend, listen to me. Carve out some time for yourself each day. Spend a few minutes alone talking to the Lord or find a friend to join you for yoga, a long walk, or for coffee on the patio. God wants you to do this for yourself; He wants you to spend some time taking care of the greatness that He has provided to you both physically and spiritually.

As women, particularly women of color, we are often so busy taking care of the entire family, the entire girlfriend circle, the entire corporate network, and others that we often neglect ourselves. When we neglect ourselves, we allow for disease, illness, worry, fear, and depression to seep into our bodies and our souls.

Begin determining how you can carve out ten minutes a day just for you. Once you master the ten minutes, take it up a notch to twenty minutes. Before you know it, you will find the hour that you need to take care of you, and God will be so proud of you. If you spend time taking care of yourself, your skin will have a renewed glow, and your smile will be naturally wide and bright. Try this today!

PRAYER

Dear God, help me to make myself a priority. I know that You want me to spend some time taking care of myself, and I know You will give me the strength, the time, and the energy to do this if I make a small effort. Lord, I ask for Your guidance and Your protection as I venture out on this journey of taking time for myself. I have not done this before because I am always taking care of others, doing for others, and looking after others. I realize now, God, that if I do not take care of myself, I will not be any good to anyone else. Thank You, Lord, in advance for speaking to me during this journey and helping me to know and believe that You are with me. You have shown me, time and time again, that You will not leave, nor forsake me, but that You will be a few steps ahead of me during the entire journey. Amen.

Warehouse future

Modernization in all areas of trade!

Beginning of the era of s

DAY 2
MY WORRY, MY FEAR, MY ANGST

How do you lay your burdens down for God?

"Be careful for nothing, but in everything by prayer and supplication with thanksgiving let your requests be made known unto God. And the peace of God, which passeth all understanding shall keep your hearts and minds through Christ Jesus."

(PHILIPPIANS: 4:6-7)

STORY

Most of the nation was still under state stay-at-home orders due to COVID-19. It was Monday, May 25, 2020. The United of States of America (USA) was celebrating Memorial Day. By all accounts, Memorial Day is the day that the

USA celebrates the lives of those who were lost while serving in the U.S. military. The nation was fighting two pandemics simultaneously.

Ironically, on Memorial Day 2020, the nation was worried about flattening the curve of the novel coronavirus while also watching a black man being killed by a police officer. The white police officer, who was eventually charged with second degree murder and third-degree manslaughter, knelt on George Floyd's neck for eight minutes and forty-six seconds. This hit home for Lisa and for so many of her friends, colleagues, family members, neighbors, and church members.

Lisa had an eight-year old son, and she was worried for his life. Often, Lisa woke up praying over her son and worried throughout the day. Her worries ranged from wondering if he was okay at school to if he could stand up for himself to if he was making good choices. Lisa's worries got scarier as her son got older. She wondered if he could handle himself if a peer tried to intimidate him or tried to convince him to make a poor choice that could get him in trouble and how he would handle encountering a police officer who did not look at him like the human being that he was.

Lisa found herself reading every news article and listening to every news show about George Floyd because it was like watching a family member killed on video. Finally, Lisa realized that she had to lay her worries on the cross. Lisa also realized and understood that this was a battle just for God.

APPLICATION

Every woman who has a black son can empathize with to Lisa and her worries as it relates to the murder of George Floyd.

It is known by many that black women carry the weight of the world, worrying about their husbands, their sons, and their daughters. This level of worry often transfers to stress, which leads to health issues such as hypertension, stroke, and depression.

God wants His people to know that He will give them all the strength they need in the hard times. He wants you to come to Him in prayer when your circumstances begin to overwhelm and burden you. God has told you and continued to affirm that He is with you. He knows that there is a long road ahead as His people seek justice for the deaths of so many black sons and black husbands who have unfairly lost their lives to law enforcement. God does not want you to worry or be anxious; He has your journey figured out, and He will be right there with you every step of the way.

PRAYER

Dear Lord, please cover my son with all your protection, keep my daughter from any harm or danger, and walk with my husband on his journey. Lord, I know I worry too much. I often forget that I am Your child. I often ignore Your teachings about having zero fear, zero worry, and zero anxiety. I know that fear, worry, and anxiety are feelings that do not align with what You have already shown me. I know that You are with me every step of the way, and I give my family to You, Lord. I lift them up to You, and I believe that You will do exactly what You have already done and will continue to do, which is provide love, care, and layer upon layer of protection for Your children. Amen.

MY GENES, MY HISTORY, MY FUTURE

How can I take the knowledge of the past and make a brighter future?

"Can a man take fire in his bosom, and his clothes not be burned?"
(PROVERBS 6:27)

STORY

Lisa's family was extremely close. During her younger years, she spent her weekends between her two grandmothers' homes. Often, there were a few stops along the way to visit with aunts and uncles. Lisa grew up in the South, and her southern roots were deep. She embraced

traditional southern culture, including eating southern food, such as fish on Fridays or grits and shrimp. She had card-playing cousins, and her church-going family members guided the decisions and habits of her family.

Lisa's dad had fought in the Vietnam War, and as a result, he returned home with many ailments, some physical and a few mental. Any person who knew Lisa's dad before he left the states for the Vietnam War would tell you that he returned to his hometown of Atlanta, Georgia a completely different person. He often suffered from depression, nightmares, anxiety, headaches, and drug addiction. Lisa witnessed all these behaviors growing up. Even as a child, she would pray to God to deliver her Dad from such sadness.

There were, indeed, some happy moments and some delightful times Lisa remembers fondly her Dad going all out for Christmas, showing up at her track practices, and cheering her on at graduations, but she was very much aware of when her dad would wallow in his sadness. If there were a heightened amount of sadness, he would indulge in drugs, and often when the "high" wore off, there would be more sadness, heightened anger, and anxiety.

Lisa vowed never to disrupt her mental health with drugs. She made a fierce effort no to t ever indulge.

APPLICATION

Sis, what do you come from? Do you have a deep-rooted issue in your family that you are fighting today? Many of our families have some level of dysfunction and illness. What is yours? Is it alcoholism, depression, drug addiction, teenage pregnancy, or name-calling? Whatever the ailment that has found a place in your family can be rebuked in the name of Jesus.

My sister, my friend, you must know that you are not alone. You have a whole team of folk who are rooting for you, encouraging you, and praying for you. Honey, you have got this! No weapon formed against you will prosper, and you must continue the good fight of telling that family ailment, "No, not today, not tomorrow, not ever. You will not control my life, and you will not live here."

P R A Y E R

Dear God, please help me, my family, my friends, and my community fight the ills of our past. Whatever ailment our families have suffered, whether it is addiction, hypertension, diabetes, anxiety, or depression, we come to You right now, dear sweet Jesus, asking You to give us the tools and the weapons to fight, so that our futures are much greater than our past. Lord, You have the power to help us to be better than what we have experienced. Your power helps to not only refuse anything that comes our way that is not good for us, but to keep ailments from even being in our presence in the first place. Lord, we thank You in advance for helping us to fight this good fight with You right by our side, leading the way to deliverance and greatness. Amen.

MY BODY, MY CHOICE, MY CONSEQUENCE

How will God chastise me for the choices that I have made?

"For I will restore health to you and heal you of your wounds."
(JEREMIAH 30:17)

STORY

Lisa was often the counselor for her girlfriend circle. She was older than her girlfriends by a few months, so they looked at her as the oldest and the wisest. One of Lisa's best girls, Sage, was extremely popular, beautiful, sociable, and often sought after by all the boys when they

were younger and many men once they entered adulthood. Lisa would often try to tell Sage that just because a guy called or wanted to take her on a date did not mean that the conversation or the date had to end in the bedroom. Sometimes Sage would listen, but oftentimes she did not.

Once Lisa and Sage were well into their adult lives, they had debates about what men were worthy of date, how the date should end, and whether there should be a second date. Sage would try to convince Lisa that each guy was "it" and that he would be her husband in a few months, no less than a year. Of course, the relationships did not end that way; they would usually end with Sage having a broken heart. Sage had developed several illnesses that were a result of having unprotected sex with more men than whose names she could remember.

APPLICATION

My dear, sweet sister, please learn from your experiences, and try your best not to repeat the mistakes of your past. Every man that asks for your phone number or asks you for a date is not worthy of your mental space, not worthy of you giving him your body, and simply not worthy of your time. As you continue this dating journey, date with discernment, and ask God to lead you and guide your decision-making.

Your body is priceless, as you are made of rubies and gold. God wants you to know just how sacred your mind, your spirit, and your body are. He created a unique and special you. You must know your worth and your value.

PRAYER

Dear God, help me to approach the dating scene with care and love for myself. Help me to know how worthy I am, dear Jesus. Lord, I ask that You show up in my conversation, in my dress, and in my behavior, so that any man that I encounter understands that I love You and that I am trying to create a life that makes you proud. I pray that I approach all decisions with my mental, spiritual, and physical health at the center. Lord Jesus, I ask for forgiveness. If I have caused any ill will toward myself or anyone else through the dating process, I ask for forgiveness. My love for You, God, is greater than that for any man, and I vow to make You proud with the decisions that I make moving forward. Lord, I thank You for second chances. Amen.

DAY 5

MY PRAYER, MY DESIRE, MY SACRIFICE

How will I sacrifice in order to have what I deserve according to God's Word?

"And thou shalt love the Lord thy God with all thy heart, and with all thy soul, and with all thy mind, and with all thy strength; this is the first commandment."

(MARK 12:30)

STORY

Lisa was a beautiful, free-spirited girl who always seemed to have the best of everything. To others, it appeared that she came from the best family and had some of the best experiences. Lisa was fortunate enough to travel extensively with her family as a child, often missing major school functions that all the kids were looking forward to for a planned family cruise or a quick family weekend getaway. As Lisa grew up and began to create a life of her own, the outward appearance of her life being perfect continued. The observations that others had of Lisa were that she had no reason to worry, as all things seemed to fall into place for her with little effort on her part.

The public opinion of Lisa was far from the truth. She worried often about her physical health and her ability to live a life that made her proud and happy. As quiet as it was kept, Lisa was diagnosed with Lupus as a teenager. As a result, she often suffered from joint pain to the point of being in tears and heavy in prayer on a daily basis. She was so afraid to share her illness with others. She did not want anyone to pity her or do things for her because they felt sympathy toward her.

Lisa sacrificed many friendships and relationships because she was very afraid to let people know her suffering. She would often isolate herself for long periods. Because of her pride, she would not share her pain with others. Her wish and her desire was to have some authentic and meaningful relationships without any person feeling sorry for her during the flare-ups that would often occur at times when she least expected.

APPLICATION

Sister, are you suffering from an illness or some pain and need help from your loved ones and your girlfriends? You know who your "real" girlfriends are, and you know that they unconditionally love you. God does not want you to suffer in silence. He has surrounded you with family and friends that are there for you, and they will support you.

You have the right to pray and ask God to relieve you of the pain. You have the right to be angry at times because this is an illness that you do not understand, nor do you have any idea why you were diagnosed. God will only give you what you can bear. This is a job that is just right for Him. He will not allow you to suffer in silence. He is right there with you and He is your healer. God's desire is your desire. He will heal you; He will comfort you, and He will strengthen you. He will also support you by bringing your loved ones, family, and friends into your life, so that they can provide a circle of love and protection for you.

PRAYER

Dear Lord, You know my desire; You know my sacrifice, and You know my prayer. I pray, Lord, that I am healed of all ailments. I pray that I can allow my loved ones to be a part of my life on a daily basis, so that we can enjoy Your blessings together. Thank You, dear Jesus, for surrounding me with love, care, and nurturing. Thank You for family and thank You for friends. Lord, I know that You are in full control and that You will ensure that I am able to enjoy fully the blessings that You have prepared for me. Thank You, Lord! Thank You, Lord! Thank You, Lord! Amen.

FEBRUARY
WEEK 13

DAY 1
HEALING YOUR MIND

Who is directing your thoughts?

*"Thou wilt keep him in perfect peace,
whose mind is stayed on thee:
because he trusteth in thee."*
(ISAIAH 26:3)

STORY

Erica's life was on an upward trajectory. After college, she landed a well-paying job at a Fortune 500 Company, which she loved. Her family adored her, and her friends were there to support her every step of the way. After purchasing and settling into her first home, she could not ask for a better life.

Despite having many reasons to be excited about where she was in life, Erica was sad. Instead of meeting friends or visiting her family after work, now when she came home, she put on pajamas and spent the evening on the couch watching television. She could not sleep at night because questions about her future raced through her mind. Not sure what to say to her friends, she did not talk to them as often. On weekends, she did not bother getting out of bed.

Going through the motions of life with numbness became Erica's new normal. It appeared to others as if everything was going well for her. Internally her thoughts consumed her so much that she felt as though she were losing her mind. Her sadness overwhelmed her, and she did not know how to escape the darkness that engulfed her.

APPLICATION

Never judge a book by its cover. Just because people seem to be doing fine externally does not mean that they are actually doing fine internally. Many people in society suffer from depression, anxiety, and other mental health issues. Often times, the symptoms go ignored or unrecognized, causing those suffering from them never to seek professional help nor spiritual help from God.

The responsibilities in our lives are great. Many of us play multiple roles, including wife, mother, daughter, sister, friend, and co-worker, to name a few. Each of these roles requires us to perform a different set of responsibilities and utilize varied skill sets. Balancing these roles along with other basic responsibilities of daily life can be overwhelming at times and cause us to misplace our focus.

As Christians, we should always direct our thoughts toward God. He has already established the plan for our lives and set the path that we must travel. When life seems too much for us, we must remember that we are not required to bear our own burdens. When we feel overwhelmed and sad, God is there to assist. Therefore, instead of focusing on all that is happening around us and simply "going through the motions of life" without truly living life to the fullest, we must take our troubles to God and allow Him to answer the questions about our future and what He has in store for us.

Confidently, I say that God's plans are to prosper you in every area of your life. He desires that you live a happy and fulfilled life. I encourage you to keep your mind on God, no matter what is happening around you. If you feel depressed and at the end of your rope, seek God and do not be afraid nor ashamed to seek professional help. He will keep you in perfect peace.

PRAYER

Dear Lord, help me to focus my mind on You at all times during all situations. Let me not become consumed and overwhelmed by life's challenges. Please do not allow sadness and hopelessness to overtake me. Help me to be all that You have called me to be as I serve all of those who have been assigned to my life. Lord, because You have already established my path, You know what lies before me. Give me the courage and the strength to depend totally on You. It is my desire to keep my mind stayed on You and to live under the covering of Your perfect peace. In the name of Jesus, Amen.

DAY 2

HEALING YOUR BODY

Do you set aside time for self-care?

*"He giveth power to the faint; and to them that have no might he increaseth strength. Even the youths shall faint and be weary, and the young men shall utterly fall: But they that wait upon the L*ORD *shall renew their strength; they shall mount up with wings as eagles; they shall run, and not be weary; and they shall walk, and not faint."*

(ISAIAH 40:29-31)

STORY

After experiencing depression for almost three months, Erica finally called out to God for the strength to gain control of her life again. Needless to say, He was there to answer

her prayers. God directed her to release all her sadness and allow Him to replace it with joy. She cast all her cares upon Him, and her load felt lighter than it ever had.

Three months later, Erica shared with her women's group at church that God had healed her mind from depression and that she had sought counseling as well. She was leery about exposing this because so many people here did not believe in counseling, but God instructed her to tell the whole story. He wanted people to know that they should explore every avenue possible to obtain the help that they need.

At the end of Erica's testimony, Sheila came over and shared that she was physically exhausted. Her doctor had recently informed her that she suffered from a lung condition. Erica immediately began to pray with Shelia for God's healing. At the end of the prayer, Erica reminded Sheila of God's healing power, emphasizing that she was a living example of it. She told Sheila that God is not a respecter of persons. Just as God healed her mind, He could also heal Sheila's body and give her strength.

APPLICATION

Unfortunately, we often neglect ourselves. We are so busy taking care of responsibilities at work, home, church, and in the community that we do not take care of our own health and wellness. We miss appointments with doctors, forget to take medications, and never stop to rest. Constantly operating in overdrive and paying little attention to our bodies will eventually take a toll and often result in physical fatigue and health issues.

Our bodies are God's temple! We must care for them in a manner that is pleasing to God. We must take time to practice healthy habits to maintain strength in our bodies. Yes, sickness will come, but when possible, we must do our part in preventing it. If for some reason our bodies experience sickness in any form, we must remember that the God we serve has healing power. Call on His name. Believe in His power and let the will of the Lord be done in your life.

Do not limit yourself to only calling on God when there is a major issue in your body, such as cancer or other types of diseases. The God you serve performs miracles big and small. He will heal for your headaches, body aches, burns, and bruises. He will heal you from exhaustion and increase your strength and stamina to continue the race. Never place God in the boxes that you have set up in your mind. He is far bigger and much greater. He operates outside of any of the parameters that you have set. Let God be God!

PRAYER

Father, there are days when I feel as if I am at the end of my rope. My body is tired and weak from the constant going and coming that I do daily to keep my life on track. Forgive me, Lord, for not taking some time to focus on me. When I am tired and sick, I am not in a position to function at my highest level nor to complete the tasks that You have assigned to me. I ask, Father, that You teach me how to practice self-care. My body is Your temple, and I want to treat it with care. Renew my strength, my God, when I am weak and burdened. Thank You in advance for activating Your healing power in every area of my life where it is needed. I trust You, God, to see me through every situation. In Jesus' name, I pray, Amen.

DAY 3

HEALING YOUR SPIRIT

Why is your soul troubled?

"Heal me, LORD, and I will be healed;
save me and I will be saved,
for you are the one I praise."
(JEREMIAH 17:14)

STORY

Although Erica overcame her bout with depression, she still did not feel like herself. Her thoughts were now clear, but her spirit was troubled. She wondered why she was so unsettled.

Erica decided to go on a fast in effort to gain clarity.

In addition to giving up food, Erica also gave up television and social media. She did not want any distractions. Her goal was to seek God and discover why she felt troubled. Each day she spent hours praying and reading the Bible.

On the fourth day of the fast, Erica heard God speak to her spirit. He told her that her spirit was troubled because her relationship with Him was not as strong as it had been in the past. When God first delivered her from depression, she remained close to Him. As time passed, instead of clinging to him, she began to go back to her normal routine and, as a result, spent less and less time with Him. Fearful of going back down that same path, Erica vowed to strengthen her relationship with God. As she began to make God the first priority in her life, He healed her spirit, and she no longer felt unsettled.

APPLICATION

Our spirits yearn for God because He is our source of everything. When we stray away from Him, we feel uneasy and unsettled in our spirits. These feelings are signs that we are not as connected to God as we were at one time. Our strained or weak connection allows troubles and issues to arise and limits our knowledge of how to respond to the situations we face. God will heal our troubled spirits when we connect to Him as our source.

The more connected we are to God, the more settled we are in our spirits. When we are strongly connected to God, He speaks to our spirits constantly, giving us instructions, warnings, knowledge, and wisdom. When our connection is weak, we do not hear Him as clearly, and we often make mistakes and wrong decisions.

Always keep God first. Never allow your family, your job, or your friends to invade the time that you have designated to commune with God and keep your spirit connected to Him. It is through your connection to God that you learn of the plans that He has for your life and the path you must follow to reach your purpose in life. Even when you stray, heed to the rumblings in your spirit, which will lead you back to Him.

P R A Y E R

Lord, I thank You for being my source. You are my joy and my peace in times of sadness and distress. You protect me from the hurt, harm, and danger that come into my life. God, teach me to recognize when I have strayed away from You. Teach me to recognize that my spirit is not settled when I am not connected to You. I seek to commune with You, oh Lord, to hear Your voice, and to follow Your lead. Give me the strength to balance my life without ever neglecting my designated time to spend with You. I need You in my life always, for all seasons and for all reasons. In the name of Jesus, I pray, Amen.

DAY 4

HEALING YOUR HEART

Have you released the hurt?

"Peace I leave with you, my peace I give unto you:
not as the world giveth, give I unto you.
Let not your heart be troubled,
neither let it be afraid."
(JOHN 14:27)

STORY

Erica felt good about herself because her mind and spirit were now in tune with God. Excited about her blossoming relationship with her new boyfriend Todd, she quickly changed into something nice for her impromptu dinner date with him. The two of them had been dating six months, and everything was going well.

Todd had all the traits that she had prayed for in a mate. He was honest, kind, considerate, compassionate, respectful, and a great listener. Passionate about his career and goals in life, Todd loved God, his family, and Erica. Convinced she would one day marry Todd, Erica often imagined their lives together in the future.

When Erica entered the restaurant to meet Todd, he was in the bar area waiting for her in his normal spot. This time, however, he was engrossed in conversation with a beautiful young woman. As Erica approached, she could hear some of their conversation.

"We always had a great time together. I can't believe how much time has passed," said the mystery woman.

"I know," Todd responded. "We have not seen each other in forever. One day soon, we should hook up."

Stunned by what she heard, Erica shouted, "How could you, Todd?" as she ran out of the restaurant in tears.

APPLICATION

Many times, we react and respond to situations without knowing all the details. Obviously, Erica assumed that Todd was having an inappropriate conversation with the young woman in the bar. He was not. The woman he was talking to was his sister's childhood friend. They were simply reminiscing about their childhood and catching up with the details of each other's lives. The two of them never said nor did anything inappropriate.

In this situation, Erica allowed past experiences and hurt dictate her actions in the present. Todd had never given her a reason to doubt his loyalty and commitment to their relationship. The automatic hurt she felt when seeing Todd talk with his childhood friend stemmed from a series of cheating incidents in a previous relationship that left her heartbroken. She had never resolved the hurt this caused, and it developed into her being insecure and mistrusting.

Any unresolved hurt that we have in our hearts manifests in other areas of our lives in one form or another. We have to learn to let go of our baggage. Carrying around old hurts weighs heavily on our hearts and hinders our forward movement. These hurts cause us to be stuck in a place of pain, and everything we say and do emanates from that pain. Instead of being open, we close ourselves off behind the walls that we have built, convinced that we will be hurt again. If we release the pain, we can embrace the new and exciting opportunities that God has planned for our lives.

PRAYER

Lord, those who have claimed to love me have hurt me deeply. The pain caused by them has blocked my ability to love freely because I am afraid of being hurt again. Father, please remove this hurt from my heart. Help me to release the pain that I have been carrying. My heart is heavy, and I need my load lightened. I want to be excited about my future. I want to live a life of expectancy, a life where I am willing to share freely my thoughts and feelings with others. In Your Word, You promised to protect me. I desire to walk in the knowledge that I have nothing to fear because You will forever be with me. Thank You, God, for my new heart that freely receives and freely gives. Amen.

DAY 5
HEALING YOUR RELATIONSHIPS

Have you extended an olive branch?

*"Confess your faults one to another,
and pray one for another, that ye may be healed.
The effectual fervent prayer of a righteous man
availeth much."*

(JAMES 5:16)

STORY

Todd excused himself from the conversation with his childhood friend Lisa and found Erica in her car, crying hysterically. Confused, he asked Erica what was wrong. With tears in her eyes, she immediately accused him of cheating, asking what had she done to deserve such treatment. Todd tried to explain the situation.

He offered to introduce Erica to Lisa, which he had planned to do anyway when she arrived. Frazzled by the incident, Erica refused to go back into the restaurant. Instead, she drove away.

Later that evening, Todd appeared at Erica's door. When she opened it, he said that he was there to make sure she had made it home safely because she had not answered any of his calls. He asked if he could come in so that they could talk. During their conversation, Erica apologized for her behavior and shared with Todd how her past relationship had influenced her reaction. He assured her that he was committed to their relationship and asked her not to treat him as if he were her last boyfriend. Erica agreed. Todd immediately forgave Erica, and they moved on.

APPLICATION

People tell us all the time that communication is a key aspect of every relationship. When we openly communicate with our spouses, children, family members, friends, and even professional associates, we minimize the potential for misunderstandings and hurt feelings. We cannot assume that anyone knows what we are thinking and feeling, nor can we blame someone for offending us when we never expressed that a particular behavior is offensive to us.

When we offend someone or someone offends us, it is important to have a conversation about the incident before it develops into something greater. Sometimes, we feel like having a conversation is not worth the effort, but it is. In having these conversations, we must remember to take ownership of the role that we may have played in the situation and be willing to listen to the other person's concerns. In other words, it needs to be two-way conversation, one that is open and honest.

Acknowledging our faults to others allows us to confess, and it allows them to forgive. Both of these acts are critical in our relationships with God. The Bible teaches us to confess our sins as well as forgive those who have sinned against us. Once we have difficult conversations about our conflicts with others, we should pray for one another and turn the situations over to God. If it is His will, God will heal the relationship so that everyone can move forward.

PRAYER

Father, thank You for giving me the strength to confess my faults to others so that they may forgive me and so that my conscious will be clear. I ask that I have a forgiving spirit and forgive those I feel have caused me hurt and pain. Teach me to be a better communicator in all my relationships, even my relationship with You. I want to feel confident in expressing my thoughts and feelings without being afraid of how others will receive my truth. Thank You, God, for forgiving me of my sins and teaching me how to forgive others. Help me to maintain healthy relationships with everyone in my life, and to remove myself from relationships that are not good for me or are not pleasing in Your sight. In the name of Jesus, I pray, Amen.

BIOS

Stephanie Perry Moore – General Editor

Stephanie Perry Moore is the trailblazing author of the Payton Skky Series, the first African American, Christian teen series. She has written over 60 titles for children and adults. In addition to writing her own titles, she is the General Editor of several Bible products. Some of the releases include *Men of Color Study Bible*, *Wisdom and Grace Bible for Young Women of Color*, and the *Women of Color Devotional Bible*. Other titles that will be released this year are *Strength and Honor Bible for Young Men of Color*, *Women of Color Cookbook*, *Wisdom and Grace Devotional Bible*, and the *African-American Family Bible*. She is the Co-Editor of REAL, an urban BibleZine published by Thomas Nelson and the Co-Founder of the Sister's in Faith brand. She speaks in schools across the nation, uplifting youth. She lives in the greater Atlanta, Georgia area with her husband, Derrick Moore. They have three young adults. Visit her website at www.stephanieperrymoore.com

Sherryll Atkins – Week 1 - Obedience

Sherryll Atkins is a screenwriter who has written for television and is currently venturing into feature films. Her reading palette includes The Bible, biblical and Hebrew history, as well as young adult fantasy literature. One of her goals is to become a published author in the young adult genre. She lives in Northern California.

First Lady Jamell Meeks – Week 2 - Virtue

First Lady Jamell Meeks is the Director of Women's Ministries for the Salem Baptist Church of Chicago under the leadership of her husband, Reverend James T. Meeks. Women of Influence serves over 4,000 women. National Chair for First Ladies Health Initiative and leader of a national pastors' wives prayer group, First Lady Meeks has been featured in several national publications for her work with entrepreneurship, women, and health. She is a certified John Maxwell speaker and speaks to hundreds of women annually. In 2004, she developed the nationally recognized A.R.I.S.E Entrepreneur Program. The program has helped over 1,100 people start and grow their small businesses. Her mission is to inspire women of all ages to live a life grounded by faith, guided by purpose, and motivated by infinite possibilities. She resides in Chicago, Illinois with her husband. She is the mother of four children and a proud grandmother of four.

Karyn L. King – Week 3 - Overcoming

Karyn L. King, MA, LPC is a loving mother of two adolescent daughters. She is a Christian Licensed Professional Counselor, Mindset Coach, and Motivational Speaker. Karyn is the owner of Total Life Counselor, LLC (TLC) that provides group and individual counseling services to youth, adolescents, adults, couples, and families. Karyn is also the creator of *Millennium Wife*, a social media life group for all women. This platform provides support, encouragement, practical development tips and advice for women in their businesses, family life, relationships as well as in their personal growth and development. She loves people and has a compassionate personality that fosters good rapport with people from all walks of life. A breast cancer survivor and an advocate for those currently battling this disease, Karyn is honored to share her life's calling, experience, training, and heart with those who seek positive change.

Dr. Christine Jenkins – Week 4 - Faithfulness

Christine Jenkins, M.Ed., is an educator and school-based administrator with years of experience working with children, youth, and families in school, judicial, and community settings. She has written articles for educational journals and served as an editor for student textbooks. She is a member of Delta Sigma Theta Sorority, Inc. and is a past director of its Southern Region. A visionary woman of faith, she loves sharing words of encouragement and hope with other women. Christina lives in Pensacola, Florida with her husband, Robert, and enjoys cooking, traveling, and spending time with her two adult daughters, son-in-law, and two grandchildren.

Brionna S. Jones – Week 5 - Self-Esteem

Brionna S. Jones is an administrative assistant at a Historically Black College and University (HBCU) who enjoys reading and writing in her spare time. She attended James Madison University and graduated from East Coast Polytechnic Institute University (formerly ECPI) in Office Technology. As a former church secretary, Sunday School teacher and Vacation Bible School teacher, she enjoys doing God's work. A former member of three choirs, she enjoys listening to and singing gospel music. Adamant about exalting the name of our Lord and Savior, Jesus Christ, she believes in encouraging and uplifting people as well as praying for them wherever she goes. Brionna is a native of Newport News, Virginia.

Mayah Emerson – Week 6 - Planting

Mayah Emerson is a graduate of Mississippi State University where she earned a bachelor's degree in educational psychology and served in many capacities, including as the first African American female Student Body President in the university's history. She is also a graduate of Brown University, where she earned a master's degree in urban education policy. As a product of public schooling in one of the poorest states in the union, Mississippi, and a first-generation college student, Mayah deeply understands the power that education has in enhancing one's trajectory. She believes that this nation has a responsibility to ensure that every American has equal access to this power. Mayah has committed her studies and career to dissecting the practices and policies that govern our education system. Her desire is to ensure that all have equal access to a quality education. Aside from her work and studies, she is a sweet tea connoisseur and political enthusiast. Mayah is a proud native of Meridian, Mississippi.

First Lady Sonya Peters Bailey – Week 7 – Wonder

Sonya Peters Bailey is a native of Brockton, Massachusetts. She developed a love for reading at a young age and has an interest in many forms of literature. She published her first article at the age of thirteen and has contributed to several Caribbean publications. Sonya is a gifted educator who has a passion for working with young people. She is a dedicated pastor's wife who loves shopping, traveling, and spending time with her family. She graduated from Gordon College and matriculated at the University of Massachusetts in the Master of Education program. Sonya lives in Connecticut with her husband and daughter.

Dr. Lakeba Hibbler Williams – Week 8 – Redemption

Dr. Lakeba Hibbler Williams is a Licensed Professional Counselor (LPC) and a National Certified Counselor (NCC) with a Bachelor of Science degree in Social Work from Southern University A&M College in Baton Rouge, Louisiana, a Master of Education degree in Community Agency Counseling, and a Doctor of Philosophy degree in Adult Education, both from Auburn University in Auburn, Alabama. She has extensive training in counseling clients suffering from the devastating effects of childhood abuse and trauma. Her mission is to teach clients healthier, more effective ways to cope with depression, anxiety, family conflict, relationship issues, and grief. Owner/Director of Fresh Hope Counseling Center, LLC. She also works part-time with the City of Atlanta's Psychological Services/Employee Assistance Program as a Behavioral Health Specialist. An author, educator, and consultant with over 25 years of experience, she is passionate about psychoeducation as well as mental health and wellness. She also serves as a speaker and workshop leader on a variety of topics, including mental health and wellness, healthy relationships, and leadership. She has presented at global, national, and regional events for universities, churches, and corporations. An active volunteer in her community, she lives in in Decatur, Georgia with her family.

Donielle Dixon – Week 9 – Makeover

Donielle Dixon is a recent college graduate of Alabama State University where she received her Bachelor of Science degree in Political Science. Donielle was involved in numerous organizations as a collegiate. She was a part of the Hornet Tribune Newspaper staff, HOST, Residential Assistant, NAACP, Collegiate 100, National Society of Leadership and Success, College Democrats, Pi Sigma Alpha, URGE, and Student Government Association Treasurer. She will be continuing her education at Northwestern University in Evanston, Illinois where she is pursuing a Master of Arts in Public Policy and Administration. Donielle loves traveling and spending time with her family. She lives in the greater Atlanta area.

Joe Ann Oatis – Week 10 - Refuge

Joe Ann Oatis is a retired music educator from the Baltimore County Public School (BCPS) system. She is the founder and director of The Boys Choir of Powhatan, a group for African American males. She also organized an after-school program for girls to promote the arts, education, physical and mental health, and social and political awareness. Joe Ann is founder and CEO of The Sitao Corporation, an independent non-profit 501(c) (3) corporation designed to provide support and services to the BCPS. Immediate past president of the Baltimore Metropolitan Alumnae Chapter of Delta Sigma Theta Sorority, Inc., Ms. Oatis was raised in Hattiesburg, Mississippi. She holds a bachelor's degree in music education from Jackson State University and completed graduate studies in music education at Morgan State University. She also holds an Advanced Professional Certification for the State of Maryland. Joe Ann lives in Maryland.

Sydni Moore – Week 11 - Prayer

Sydni Moore is a multimedia journalist for WFXG Fox 54 News in Augusta, Georgia. She is a 2019 graduate of a Mississippi State University with a Bachelor of Arts degree in Broadcast Journalism. As a collegiate, she was the news anchor for the Hail State

News Show, the Director of the Football Recruiting Ambassadors, Vice President of the Nu Beta chapter of Delta Sigma Theta, Inc., and a volunteer for Habitat for Humanity. She is the co-author of *Anything I want to Be*. A member of Joybells Christian gospel group that released a children's CD for Urban Spirit Publishers, Sydni has a passion to tell news stories that inspire. She lives in Augusta, Georgia.

Shea Stephens – Week 12 - Gratitude

Shea Stephens is an educator and active member of her church. She enjoys spending time with her family and friends as well as sharing her personal trials and triumphs to encourage others. At church, she serves in many capacities, including Youth Department member, President of the Women's Ministry, Touch of Grace Dance Ministry member, Children's Church Teacher, OSBBC Gospel Choir member, and Deaconess. She likes to spend her summers traveling with her family. Shea lives in North Augusta, South Carolina with her husband and three children.

Tia McCollors – Week 13 - Thankful

Tia McCollors is a bestselling author, speaker, and writing coach. Her first Christian novel, *A Heart of Devotion*, was an Essence Magazine bestseller. Other bestselling titles followed, including *Zora's Cry*, *The Last Woman Standing*, and *Steppin' Into The Good Life*. Her Days of Grace Series (*Friday Night Love*, *Sunday Morning Song* and *Monday Morning Joy*) continues to grow in popularity. In addition to ten novels, Tia has penned several non-fiction projects, including a devotion titled, *If These Shoes Could Talk*. When she is not writing, Tia finds passion in delivering inspiring and faith-based messages to women about how to maximize their lives. Her enthusiastic messages encourage women to embrace their true calling, journey through life with purpose, and cultivate the confidence and dedication to meet their goals. Tia and her husband, Wayne, live with their three children in the greater Atlanta area.

Essie M. Jeffries – Week 14 - Restoration

Essie M. Jeffries is a retired Los Angeles County Deputy Probation Officer and an American Airlines customer service agent. She received her Master of Arts degree from California State University, Los Angeles. Essie viewed education as an approach to having a successful life. She has served as president of several organizations, chaired many prosperous fundraisers and been a member of several foundation boards. Essie has been featured in *Occasion to Savory*, a major cookbook, and *My Sisters Story*, fictional stories of a group of Delta Sigma Theta Sorority, Inc. women. She enhanced her Christian life through a two-year course in evangelism and graduated in the top 5% of her class. Essie can be found every Sunday in Sunday School and then church service at Atherton Baptist Church in Hawthorne, California. She attends women's Bible study on Thursday nights. Essie never thought when she was learning more about the goodness of God that she was preparing herself to pen words in this daily devotion. She lives in Los Angeles, California with her husband and family.

LaTonyar Robinson – Week 15 - Mercy

LaTonyar Robinson is a Division I football coach's wife. In this role, she and her husband have ministered to student athletes for over twenty years. She is a member of Alpha Kappa Alpha Sorority, Inc. and volunteers for many charitable organizations. She and her husband live in Texas, where he coaches for Texas A&M University. They have two adult children.

Dr. Tina Maria Harris – Week 16 - Listening

Dr. Tina M. Harris is a professor and devout woman of faith who is a worshipper at heart. She is a lifelong educator and the nation's first endowed chair of race, media, and cultural literacy. Her first time contributing to a devotional, Tina is dedicated to promoting social justice issues through her profession and every other facet of her life. She enjoys time with her family and friends, cooking, national and international travel, learning about other cultures, singing, reading, writing, and much more. She lives in Baton Rouge, Louisiana with her dachshund-beagle mixed named Bullitt.

Kayla A. Monroe – Week 17 - Preparation

Kayla A. Monroe, MBA is a young professional in corporate America who loves pushing the envelope to get people to be comfortable with the uncomfortable. She grew up in a Christian household and is now enjoying her twenties learning, loving, and finding God for herself. Figuring out this thing called "adulting," she enjoys anything relaxing from laying out on the beach in different countries to knitting and watching Netflix! As an aspiring philanthropist, Kayla has her hands in many volunteering efforts ranging from weekly English tutoring sessions with inner city 1st graders to frequently providing workshops to local young women, teaching them the importance of personal finance, to her favorite—building houses with Habitat for Humanity around the world! She lives in Enfield, Connecticut.

Pastor Dr. Billie Boyd-Cox – Week 18 - Jesus

Dr. Billie Boyd-Cox serves as the pastor of Macedonia Baptist Church, Conyers, Georgia. The first woman to serve as pastor of a historic African American Baptist Church in Rockdale County, she currently serves on the Board of Directors for Phoenix Pass and is the recipient of numerous awards and citations. Dr. Cox earned a Bachelor of Science degree, summa cum laude, in Organizational Leadership from Mercer University, a Master of Divinity degree from McAfee School of Theology, and a Doctor of Ministry degree, summa cum laude, from the Interdenominational Theological Center. She is also a graduate of Leadership Rockdale. A realtor, founder of Open Door Ministries International, and CEO of Beyond the Walls Coaching and Consulting, LLC, she is the author of three books. Dr. Cox resides in Oxford, Georgia with her family.

Melissa Teemer Mims – Week 19 - Joy

Melissa Teemer Mims is a businesswoman and a humanitarian at heart. She enjoys advocating, motivating, and encouraging others to reach their full potential mentally, physically, and spiritually. A strong believer in building a prosperous and sustainable community though service, she has been recognized as a leading lady for her strong community involvement. She earned her Bachelor of Arts degree from Savannah State University and Master of Arts degree in psychology with a specialty in Organizational Development from The University of the Colorado, Rockies. Melissa is the creator of "I am that Parent" group on Facebook. She currently serves as a human trafficking coordinator and director of Showtime Pro, Inc. Melissa lives by the motto, "She believed she could, so she did!" Melissa resides in the greater Atlanta area with her three children.

First Lady Mona D. Thomas – Week 20 - Commitment

Mona D. Thomas, First Lady of Living Word Community Church of Los Angeles, has been serving in this capacity for twenty-one years. She enjoys family time, cooking, reading, and dancing. She is passionate about encouraging women of all ages whenever the opportunity presents itself and ministering to families experiencing grief due to death, illness and/or separation. She is an entrepreneur, a part-time Haz-Mat Specialist at FedEx, and served as the program coordinator for the Culturally Based Algebra Camp for the last decade. Mrs. Thomas is the wife of the Rev. Dr. James M. Thomas, and together, they have four children, all currently studying at the university and medical school levels. Born and raised in St. Louis, Missouri, when she married, she moved to Southern California where she has lived for twenty-eight years.

First Lady Kelli Ann Jones – Week 21 – Dreams

Kelli Ann Jones hales from Southern Illinois. She came to know the Lord as a child through the loving guidance of an aunt. While pursuing her undergraduate degree in education at Trinity International University, she met her husband, Watson. They currently live in Chicago, Illinois where Watson serves as a senior pastor. They have three beautiful children. Kelli currently works as a special education teacher.

Rev. Dr. Twanna Henderson – Week 22 – Rising

Rev. Dr. Twanna Henderson co-founded New Beginnings Church in Matthews, NC with her husband, Rev. Dr. Michael L. Henderson, Sr. A devoted wife and mother of a special needs son, she is a Bible teacher, preacher, and author. Dr. Henderson has a Bachelor of Arts degree in Communications from the University of North Carolina at Chapel Hill and a Juris Doctorate degree from North Carolina Central University in Durham, North Carolina. She studied at Gordon Conwell Theological Seminary in the Master of Christian Leadership program, and she holds an Honorary Doctorate of Divinity from St. Thomas Christian University in Jacksonville, Florida. A licensed attorney, she served thirteen years as a Civil Court Magistrate Judge for Mecklenburg County in Charlotte, North Carolina. She is the owner of Twanna Henderson Ministries (www. TwannaHenderson.com), which provides a virtual Master Class Coaching and Mentoring program. In the fall of 2013, she published her first book, *Dancing with the Scars*.

Pastor Tracy Smith Williams – Week 23 – Hospitality

Tracy Smith Williams, MBA is the founder of Wonder Women's Experience, the women's ministry at The Spirit Church in St. Louis, Missouri, where she pastors alongside her husband. Tracy has a heart for teen girls. She shares her abstinence program "The Garden Experience" in schools, ministries, and other organizations. She enjoys watching movies, spending time with her family, and people watching! She and her husband Aeneas have four children and live in Creve Coeur, Missouri.

Nicole Brewington Smith – Week 24 – Heart

Nicole Brewington Smith, MBA is a mother of three young men, an educator, and a seasoned woman of faith. She enjoys writing, especially when she has the opportunity to encourage women. This is her second set of published devotionals. The first set can be found in the *Women of Color Devotional Bible*. Smith is a breast cancer survivor and generously volunteers her time to educate communities of color about healthy behaviors. She enjoys traveling, working out, and dining out. She is able to indulge in her three favorite past times now that she is an empty nester. It is her prayer that women will read the words she has penned and continue to move forward to be all that God has called them to be. Smith lives in the Kansas City metropolitan area.

Dr. LaQuanda Carpenter – Week 25 – Health

Dr. LaQuanda Carpenter has served in the education field for more than 20 years in Georgia and Missouri, working in all settings, K-12. Dr. Carpenter is a highly skilled school leader, public speaker, and visionary. She has experience in traditional public schools, public-charter schools, and private schools. Dr. Carpenter has expertise in student and staff empowerment, teacher development and leadership, school transformation and turn-around, inclusion, equity, and databased decision-making. As a school principal, Dr. Carpenter has been an advocate for ensuring that all students within a school building are treated with dignity, respect, love, and care. Furthermore, she often shares educational, historical, and political viewpoints as a youth and women's empowerment speaker. Dr. Carpenter lives in the Kansas City, Missouri area with her husband, Dr. Dennis L. Carpenter, and their two young children.

Dr. Charrita Danley Quimby – Week 26 – Healing

Dr. Charrita Danley Quimby is an author, editor, publisher, and educator. Founder of Chideria Publishing, Inc., she provides writing, editing and publishing services to a broad range of clients. Passionate about creating stories, Charrita is the author of the novel, *Through the Crack,* which chronicles a family's struggle to overcome drug addiction. She has written and edited numerous manuscripts, reports, grants, and other materials for individuals and organizations. In addition, she conducts presentations and workshops on various topics. A member of Delta Sigma Theta Sorority, Inc., she attended Tougaloo College, Louisiana State University, and Georgia State University, earning the Bachelor of Arts, Master of Arts, and Doctor for Philosophy degrees in English, respectively. A native of Mississippi, Charrita is married to Dr. Ronald Quimby, and their family includes one son and two daughters.

GOALS

Become an US Urban Spirit! Publishing and Media Company
Independent or Church Distributor Today!

- earn extra money
- engage with more people
- change lives
- join a winning team
- distribute high-quality Bibles and books

Go to www.urbanspirit.biz

Order your Independent or Church Distributor
"Starter Kit" today online. It contains everything you need
to get started selling right away.
Or call **800.560.1690** to get started today!

KING JAMES VERSION

WOMEN COLOR
STUDY BIBLE